THE COMPLETE GUIDE TO DOBERMAN PINSCHERS

Tarah Schwartz

Publication Data

Doberman Pinschers

The Complete Guide to Doberman Pinschers – First edition.

Summary: "Successfully raising a Doberman Pinscher Dog from puppy to old age" – Provided by publisher.

ISBN: 978-1-952069-87-1

[1. Doberman Pinschers – Non-Fiction] I. Title.

This book has been written with the published intent to provide accurate and author-itative information in regard to the subject matter included. While every reasonable precaution has been taken in preparation of this book the author and publisher expressly disclaim responsibility for any errors, omissions, or adverse effects arising from the use or application of the information contained inside. The techniques and suggestions are to be used at the reader's discretion and are not to be considered a substitute for professional veterinary care. If you suspect a medical problem with your dog, consult your veterinarian.

Design by Sorin Rădulescu

First paperback edition, 2021

TABLE OF CONTENTS

CHAPTER 18

CHAPTER 19

CHAPTER 1

The History of the Doberman Pinscher

The Origins of the Doberman Pinscher

Although there is some dispute on the origins of the Doberman Pinscher, many experts suggest that the breed was first created in the 1880s by a tax collector named Karl Friedrich Louis Dobermann. In addition to his work as a tax collector, Dobermann also ran a dog pound in Apolda, Germany. His work gave him access to a variety of breeds, which he combined in his quest to create a breed that could protect him as a tax collector. He desired a dog with impressive stamina, strength, and intelligence. Dobermann used terriers for their quick reaction time, and he used guarding and herding breeds for their power and intelligence. It's believed that the Beauceron, German Pinscher, Rottweiler, and Weimaraner all contributed to the creation of the breed. After Dobermann's death in 1894, a fellow breeder named Otto Goeller created the National Doberman Pinscher Club and continued to perfect and refine the breed until it resembled the modern Doberman.

Though the Doberman Pinscher was named in honor of its creator, many kennel clubs around the world have since dropped the name 'pinscher,' as this is the German word for terrier and is no longer appropriate for the breed. Currently, the US and Canada are the only countries that continue to use the Pinscher name and have also dropped the second 'n' from the creator's surname.

The Doberman was first recognized by the American Kennel Club in 1908, though

FUN FACT

Doberman Pinscher Club of America

The Doberman Pinscher Club of America (DPCA) was founded in 1921 and is a national nonprofit organization based out of Michigan. The DPCA is the only officially American Kennel Club (AKC) recognized club for this breed. Membership with the DPCA offers numerous voting benefits, as well as access to the club newsletter, "The Pipeline." For more information about the club or membership inquiries, visit dpca.org.

*Photo Courtesy
of Samantha Whited
Premier Dobermans*

Photo Courtesy of Brooklyn Burnz

the breed remained relatively rare until the 1920s. The Doberman Pinscher Club of America was founded in 1921 by breeder George Earle III. After the club's formation, Earle and a group of fellow Doberman fanciers adopted a breed standard that was first developed by German breeders. By 1934, over 1,000 Dobermans were registered each year, and the following year, the first American breed standard was implemented and approved by the American Kennel Club. The breed continued to rise in popularity, and in 1939, Ch. Ferry v Raufelsen of Giralda became the first Doberman to win Best in Show at the Westminster Kennel Club Dog Show. That title was also won by Dobermans in 1952, 1953, and 1989. In 1941, the Doberman was ranked as the 15th most popular dog breed in the United States.

Throughout the 1940s, the Doberman Pinscher was used in the military and served as sentries, messengers, and scouts. These brave canine soldiers were eventually memorialized by a statue installed in Guam by the United Doberman Club. The statue, sculpted by artist Susan Bahary, was installed in 1994 in remembrance of the courageous Doberman Pinschers that gave their lives during World War II.

Doberman Pinschers have rarely been used as military dogs after World War II, as the military has focused their need for trained canines on breeds such as the Belgian Malinois and Dutch Shepherd. Since then, Doberman Pinschers have been frequently used for search and rescue due to trainability, intelligence, and keen sense of smell. Dobermans were used in search and rescue after the World Trade Center terrorist attacks in 2001.

There are still a few Dobermans being trained for military and police purposes. In Karnataka, India, a Doberman police dog named Tunga became famous. During her career, she uncovered more than 50 murders and 60 thefts and even chased a suspect over 12 kilometers before apprehending him. In 2020, Tunga was still actively working with the police, though at 10 years old she is expected to retire soon.

The Modern Doberman Pinscher

Since the development of the breed, the Doberman Pinscher has continued to win the hearts of dog lovers around the world. In 2017, the American Kennel Club ranked the Doberman as the 16th most popular dog breed.

Not only is the Doberman Pinscher loved as a devoted and affectionate family pet, but the breed is also well known for its success in the show and sport ring. Dobermans can be seen competing in nearly every dog sport.

Photo Courtesy
of Sofia Edholm

Stereotypes and Misconceptions about the Doberman Pinscher

Despite the Doberman Pinscher's loyal and affectionate nature, the breed has gained an unfortunate reputation for being vicious and aggressive. Since the breed was originally developed as a guard dog, it was created with an intimidating stature and fearless nature. The dogs needed to willingly defend their owners from attackers, whether human or canine. Though this trait served the breed well as military working dogs, modern breeders

Photo Courtesy of Maria Johnson

have toned down the aggression to create a breed that is good-natured and trainable.

The Doberman Pinscher's natural suspicion of strangers makes it an excellent guard dog, but with proper training and socialization, the breed is generally sociable toward new people and dogs as long as they do not present a threat to the Doberman's family or property.

It has been suggested that American Doberman Pinschers have a calmer and more even temperament than many of the working dogs in Europe. Differing breeding strategies have created lines of Doberman Pinschers with different temperament traits. In general, the breed is considered to be mentally stable and, with proper training and socialization, is appropriate for a family environment.

Though it's important to disregard the negative stereotypes associated with the breed, it's equally important to consider the breed's temperament when searching for a Doberman Pinscher to add to your family. This topic will be discussed in more detail in Chapter 3, but it's vital to recognize that responsible breeders prioritize a stable temperament in order to repair the damage caused to the breed by its unfortunate reputation. Less reputable breeders, however, may be willing to sacrifice temperament in favor of physical characteristics such as size and color. For the sake of the breed as a whole, it's crucial to seek out reputable breeders who intend to better the breed and repair its damaged reputation, rather than pad their pockets by breeding dogs that have not been health or temperament tested.

CHAPTER 2
The Doberman Pinscher

Physical Characteristics

Doberman Pinschers are medium- to large-sized dogs with noble and elegant appearances. They are compactly built, muscular, and square in shape. Overall, they carry themselves proudly and appear to be built for speed and great endurance. At maturity, male Dobermans are between 26 and 28 inches in height at the withers, with the ideal height at about 27.5 inches. Females should be between 24 and 26 inches at withers with an ideal height of 25.5 inches. Male Doberman Pinschers usually weigh between 75 and 100 pounds, while females weigh between 60 and 90 pounds. As the Doberman's body is square in shape, the distance from the forechest to the rear of the upper thigh should be equal in length to the dog's height.

According to the American Kennel Club's breed standard, the Doberman Pinscher's head is long and wedge shaped. The eyes are almond-shaped, moderately deep set, and have an energetic expression. In black dogs, the eyes may be medium to dark brown, while in red, blue, and fawn dogs, the color of the eyes should blend with the color of the coat. Darker colored eyes are always preferable. Black Dobermans should always have black noses, but they may be dark brown on red, dark gray on blue, and dark tan on fawn. The Doberman's jaws should be full and powerful with strongly developed teeth. The teeth should meet in a scissor bite. The ears are normally cropped for show dogs in the United States but may be left natural for pet and sport dogs. Ear cropping is a surgical

> **HELPFUL TIP**
> **Albino Doberman Pinschers**
>
> In 1976, the first recorded albino Doberman, Padula's Queen Sheba, was born. After Sheba's birth, albino or "white" Dobermans gained popularity as rare, novelty dogs. The DPCA vehemently opposes the intentional breeding of albino Dobermans, as this genetic defect can cause several health issues for the dog, including but not limited to skin cancer and photophobia. White Dobermans frequently end up in rescue shelters due to their special needs.

Photo Courtesy
of Aly Sandahl

procedure in which a veterinarian removes a portion of the dog's ear in order for it to stand erect. If left natural, the ears of the Doberman are wide and flop forward. For more information on ear cropping and tail docking, refer to Chapter 8.

The neck of the Doberman Pinscher is proudly carried, well-muscled, and well arched. It should be proportionate to both the body and head of the dog. The back should be short, of sufficient width, and straight from the withers to the croup. The Doberman's chest is broad and well defined. The front legs should be perfectly straight and parallel to each other. The belly is well tucked up and the loins are wide and muscular. In the United States, tails are docked at approximately the second joint, but are often left natural in other countries. The angulation of the hind legs should balance that of the forequarters. When the Doberman Pinscher is at rest, the line from the hock to the heel should be perpendicular to the ground. The feet of the Doberman are tight and round, often described as cat feet.

The Doberman Pinscher is a smooth-haired breed with a short, hard, thick, and close lying coat. The American Kennel Club (AKC) accepts four coat colors: black, red, blue, and fawn. Fawn coats are often referred to as Isabella. Dobermans should have rust-colored markings above each eye,

Photo Courtesy of Stephanie Johnstun

on the muzzle, throat, chest, all legs and feet, and below the tail. A white patch on the chest is permissible as long as it does not exceed ½ square inch. Dogs of any other color than those listed here will be disqualified in the show ring.

The gait of the Doberman Pinscher is often described as free, balanced, and vigorous. Dobermans should display good driving power in the hindquarters and a good reach in the forequarters. Each rear leg should move in line with the foreleg on that side, with the rear and front legs thrown neither in nor out. When in movement, the back should remain strong and firm. When correctly built Doberman Pinschers move at a fast trot in a single-track. This means that all four feet land roughly in a single line.

Behavioral Characteristics

The AKC breed standard describes the Doberman Pinscher as an energetic, watchful, and loyal breed. The dogs are often described as determined, fearless, and obedient. The temperament of the Doberman Pinscher is one of the breed's defining characteristics and is judged accordingly. In the show ring, a judge will readily dismiss any dog that displays shy or aggressive behavior. Dobermans should never shy away from the judge or fear the approach of people. Any dog that displays a vicious or belligerent attitude toward the judge or other people will not be tolerated.

Doberman Pinschers are incredibly intelligent dogs. In a study on canine intelligence performed by psychologist Stanley Coren, breeds were ranked according to their responses to obedience command training. The Doberman was ranked as the 5th most intelligent dog breed. In other studies performed throughout the 1980s, the Doberman was consistently ranked as one of the most intelligent and trainable dog breeds. Their trainability is obvious in their success in a variety of dog sports.

Photo Courtesy
of Sarah O'Neil

Doberman Pinschers as Family Dogs

"The Doberman is best suited to a family that can spend quite a bit of time with it. They love their people and want to be around them 24/7. They have received the nickname "Velcro dog" for that reason. You will never use the restroom alone again."

DENISE MORMAN
DeMor Dobermans

Doberman Pinschers are people-oriented dogs that are loyal and affectionate with their families. When properly socialized, Dobermans are also generally well-behaved around strangers. They are considered to be excellent pets and family companions and are suitable for families with young children and other pets. When raised alongside children, they are typically gentle, patient, and kind around their tiny human family members. Contrary to many stereotypes, the Doberman Pinscher makes an excellent family dog.

An active family environment is ideal for the Doberman Pinscher. As with most breeds, insufficient physical and mental stimulation can lead to destructive behavioral problems, so it's important to understand that Dobermans need plenty of activity to keep them happy and healthy. Dobermans are incredibly loyal to their families, so the more time you spend with your dog,

Photo Courtesy
of Rachael Vice

Photo Courtesy of Núria Gort Luna

the better. This is not a breed that will thrive if left outside in the yard alone. Families who regularly partake in outdoor activities such as hiking, biking, and swimming are ideal for Doberman Pinschers. This athletic and affectionate breed will happily accompany you on any adventure.

Doberman Pinschers as Working or Sport Dogs

The Doberman Pinscher's athleticism and intelligence are ideal for many working environments and dog sports. Dobermans are capable of excelling in nearly any activity, ranging from protection sports to agility to dock diving. The breed is often seen competing in obedience and flyball as well. It's not uncommon to see Dobermans competing in sports not traditionally associated with the breed, such as lure coursing, carting, and tracking.

Doberman Pinschers are also ideal for work as service and therapy dogs due to their intelligence, trainability, and alertness. They are sensitive to the needs of others and, when properly trained, can respond to the needs of their handler or those around them. A well-bred Doberman that comes from a line of temperament-tested dogs may be an ideal candidate for anyone looking for a service or therapy dog.

CHAPTER 3
Where to Find Your Doberman Pinscher

"A Doberman Pinscher is best suited for an owner who understands the breed's unique characteristics. It will need an owner that has the time and discipline to provide the training, stimulation, and daily exercise the breed requires. A minimum of two stimulating outings a day is best. By putting in the work of training, socializing, and exercising your Doberman you will be rewarded with a dog that is versatile, highly intelligent, and devoted to your family."

TRACY DOTY
Halo Dobermans

Adopting an Adult vs. Puppy

Before you begin your search for a Doberman Pinscher, it's important to know what type of dog you'd like to bring into your home. The first step is to decide whether you'd prefer to adopt a puppy or an adult dog. There are pros and cons to both.

One of the greatest benefits of adopting an adult Doberman Pinscher is that the dog will have already gone through the most obnoxious puppy stages. The destruction from teething and housetraining should already be over by the time you bring your new dog home. Additionally, many adult dogs already have some idea of the basic rules of living in a house with people and may even understand a few basic obedience commands. However, adopting an adult dog isn't always easy. Some adult dogs may not have been housetrained or ever lived indoors in previous homes. Though most shelter dogs are given up due to lifestyle changes in their households, some are given up because of the previous owner's inability to deal with health or behavioral problems.

If you decide to adopt an adult Doberman Pinscher, it's important for you and your family to decide on any problems that may be dealbreakers for you. It can be incredibly rewarding to care for a special needs dog, but it can also be a lot of work, so it's crucial for you to decide whether you're up to the challenge. Most behavioral or training issues can be overcome or managed with enough time and effort committed to the dog's training, but you'll need to decide whether that is something you and your family can handle.

Bringing home a Doberman Pinscher puppy can also present unique challenges and opportunities. In terms of training, you'll essentially be starting with a blank slate. You won't be frustrated by behavioral problems developed in previous homes, and you can train the puppy however you like. However, you'll also need to make sure that you don't allow any bad habits to develop under your watch. Puppy ownership also has frustrating aspects, such as teething. As your Doberman puppy's adult teeth come in, he may attempt to chew on furniture, shoes, and other household items in an attempt to soothe his aching gums. Additionally, you'll need to work with your new puppy on housetraining to teach him where he's allowed to relieve himself. If you're confident in your abilities as a dog trainer or are willing to work with a professional, you may feel comfortable bringing home a Doberman of any age, but it's still something to consider before you begin searching for your dream dog.

Photo Courtesy
of Samantha Whited
Premier Dobermans

Purchasing from a Breeder vs. Adopting from a Shelter

Once you have some idea of whether you'd prefer an adult Doberman Pinscher or a puppy, you'll need to further consider what characteristics you'd like in your new companion. It's essential to keep your long-term goals in mind when considering what kind of dog you'd like. If you're searching for a future show ring star or competitive sport dog, you'll have better chances of finding your ideal dog if you search for breeders. However, if you're simply searching for a loving companion for you and your family, you may be content with a dog from a shelter or breed rescue organization.

Finding your ideal Doberman Pinscher can take some time, so you'll also need to decide whether you're willing to wait for the right dog. Many breeders only have one or two litters a year, so you may be placed on a waiting list for some time. Additionally, not all areas have breed-specific rescue groups, and Dobermans aren't a common breed in shelters, so it may be somewhat of a challenge to find your perfect dog if you're in a hurry.

Purchasing a Doberman Pinscher from a reputable breeder is one of the best ways to ensure that you're bringing home a high-quality and healthy dog. Though it's a common misconception that you can only get a puppy from a breeder, many breeders have adults in need of new homes. Those adult dogs may be retired show or breeding stock, or the breeders may simply have decided to scale back their operation. As long as you purchase your new Doberman from a reputable breeder whose only desire is to improve the breed with each generation, you can be sure that you're getting a healthy dog. However, it's important to do your research before signing any contracts or agreements in order to ensure that the breeder you're working with has a good reputation. Reputable breeders will likely ask you just as many questions as you ask them to make sure that you're the right type of home for their dog.

If you're interested in giving a homeless dog the opportunity for a better life, you might consider adopting your new Doberman Pinscher from a rescue organization or shelter. However, you'll still need to research the organization as shady rescues do exist, and the animals in their possession may not receive the best care. Though most shelters don't see purebred Doberman Pinschers often, you may be able to find a breed-specific rescue in your area. Breed-specific rescues are often excellent resources to find your ideal dog as they have a better understanding of the breed and the type of home that they require.

Rescuing a Doberman Pinscher

"You should try to find a rescue organization that is able to give you a relatively detailed history of the dog, unless you are trained and prepared to deal with potential behavioral challenges. Unfortunately, the past experiences of a rescue dog are not always known and the rescue group can often only give you information regarding what they have witnessed while the dog has been in their foster care. That's not to say that really excellent dogs can't be adopted through a rescue, quite the contrary, you should just be prepared to deal with challenges should they crop up."

TRACY DOTY
Halo Dobermans

If you're interested in rescuing a Doberman Pinscher from either a local shelter or breed-specific rescue organization, it's important to understand that they may require you to undergo a bit of scrutiny before you're approved for adoption. During the application process, it's important for you to be completely honest about your home and lifestyle. Rescue staff and volunteers are not there to judge you for the way you live. They just want to make sure the animals in their care are going to loving and appropriate homes.

Most application forms will ask you about your house, family, lifestyle, and finances. Rescue staff want to ensure that dogs are matched to their ideal homes as it is stressful for dogs to be adopted only to be returned a few days or weeks later. Depending on the organization you're adopting from, it may take several days or weeks to be approved for adoption, so if there's a specific dog you had your eye on, he may already find a new home before you're approved. For this reason, many rescues recommend filling out an application as soon as possible so that you'll be preapproved should your ideal dog come into the rescue at a later time.

Many rescue organizations also require a home check, which involves a rescue staff member or volunteer visiting your home to make sure it's safe for a dog. Again, they are not there to judge your taste in décor, but instead, they want to make sure that your fencing is secure and there are no obvious dangers to a new dog. Unless the problems they find are significant, they are unlikely to deny your application then and there. Most organizations are willing to give you a chance to fix any problems so long as you're willing.

Questions to Ask Before Bringing a Doberman Pinscher Home

Before you speak to a breeder or rescue staff member about a potential adoption, you'll need to prepare a list of questions to ask before you meet the dog. It can be exciting to meet a new dog for the first time, so it's easy to forget important questions in the moment if you haven't prepared before-hand. First, you'll need to ask questions pertaining to the dog's health and history. Ask questions such as:

- Is the dog spayed or neutered?
- What vaccinations has the dog received?
- Has the dog been dewormed recently?
- Has the dog had any health problems in the past?
- Have the dog's parents undergone health testing prior to breeding? If so, what were the results?
- Has the dog itself undergone any health testing?

Once you've established that you're bringing home a healthy dog or are willing to deal with any special health needs, you can move on to questions about the dog's behavior and training. Regardless of whether you've decided to bring home an adult or puppy, it's important to establish that the dog has the right temperament for your family and your lifestyle. Here are examples of behavioral questions to ask:

- What is the dog's temperament and personality like?
- Has he/she ever shown signs of aggression?
- Is the dog overly fearful?
- Does the dog get along with other dogs?
- Is the dog cat-friendly?
- How is the dog around children?
- Is the dog housetrained?
- Does the dog know any commands? If so, which ones?
- Does the dog have any known behavioral problems or bad habits?

If you're adopting your new Doberman Pinscher from a shelter, you may also consider asking how the dog ended up there. Many times, dogs end up in rescues through no fault of their own, but if the previous owners had a problem with the dog, it's important to know about it before committing to adoption.

If you're adopting a dog from a breeder for a specific purpose, you'll also need to make sure the dog will align with your long-term goals. Not all puppies from a single litter are destined for the show or sport ring, so it's important to discuss your needs and goals with the breeder. Ask the breeder questions such as:

- Are the parents titled in any sports?
- Have siblings from previous litters gone on to compete successfully?
- Does this dog have the right conformation and temperament for a certain sport?

It can also be helpful to ask about your new Doberman Pinscher's current diet. Even if you plan on feeding something different down the line, you'll need to feed the dog his current diet for a little while so you can transition him over to the food of your choice with minimal digestive upset. Be sure to ask about any food allergies or preferences as well.

Remember, if a breeder or rescue staff member doesn't seem to answer the questions honestly or you get a bad feeling about the person or group while asking questions, it's best to walk away and find a breeder or rescue that you trust to adopt from. Reputable breeders are always more than willing to answer any questions you may have, so if you don't feel that the person is being completely transparent with you, keep searching.

Choosing a Reputable Breeder

"A responsible breeder is someone who screens both parents for health problems prior to breeding. They are dedicated to the preservation of the breed and strive to breed out hereditary problems and faults, with a mission of improving the overall breed. They are looking for qualities in a stud dog that will compliment their female so that they are producing the healthiest and conformationally correct puppies that they can. Responsible breeders screen new puppy buyers to make sure that the puppy is being put in a safe home with new owners that understand the care and training requirements of a young Doberman. A potential new owner should be prepared to answer many questions and should also have questions of their own for the breeder. The purchase of a puppy is a commitment and a responsible breeder will be a resource for you throughout the life of that dog."

TRACY DOTY
Halo Dobermans

Once you begin searching for your ideal Doberman Pinscher, it's crucial that you don't just choose a puppy from the first breeder you see in the local classifieds. To ensure that you are bringing home a healthy, well-bred, purebred dog, it's important to do your research to find a reputable breeder. If you want to begin your search on the internet, there are a few critical qualities to look for in a reputable breeder that separate them from those just looking to make money off their puppies.

FUN FACT
Doberman Movie Star

The 1946 film "It Shouldn't Happen to a Dog" features one of the earliest Doberman movie stars. Starring Carole Landis, Allyn Joslyn, and an unnamed Doberman, this post-World War II era comedy crime film follows a reporter and his comedic interludes with a mysterious woman and her dog.

The American Kennel Club offers a service on their website called the AKC Marketplace, where you can search for Doberman Pinscher breeders. Typically, the advertisements for each breeder will list the puppies they have available, if any, the price of the puppies, and expected future litters, as well as contact information. The breeders may also list their dogs' most noteworthy achievements and any breed club affiliations they may have. You'll also be able to research the pedigrees of the puppies and search for the parent dogs' health test results by inputting that information into the Orthopedic Foundations for Animals' (OFA) website. The OFA is further discussed in the next pages of this book. Additionally, the Doberman Pinscher Club of America (DPCA) has a list of breeders on their website. Though these websites are a great place to start, you'll still need to research each breeder to ensure that their reputation is as good as they claim.

One of the best ways to find a reputable Doberman Pinscher breeder is to ask other Doberman owners where they found their dogs. You might also consider attending local dog shows or sport competitions to see individual dogs in action. If you see dogs that appeal to you or match your ideal Doberman, consider asking their handlers for advice. Likewise, it's worth your time to ask about dogs that don't match your ideal pet so that you know which breeders you want to avoid. Most owners and handlers are happy to talk about their dogs and may also be willing to answer any lingering questions you may have about the Doberman before you commit to bringing one home.

Remember, a reputable breeder always prioritizes the well-being of their Dobermans over all else. With each generation, they seek to improve the health of the breed and are willing to thoroughly health test each dog before breeding them. They also strictly adhere to the breed standard and do not breed for off-standard characteristics such as disqualifying colors or sizes. Reputable breeders are extremely picky about which dogs are allowed into their breeding programs.

Good breeders will also be enthusiastic about discussing their Dobermans' performance records and titles. Though many breeders have this information published on their website, it's still worth asking about, especially if you're looking for a future show or sport dog. Even if your new dog is destined for life as an active family companion, it can be helpful to know what his background is like and the type of dogs he descends from. By bringing home a well-bred dog, you are giving him a better chance to become a polite member of the community, as long as he receives the right training.

HELPFUL TIP
Doberman Assistance, Rescue, and Education, Inc. (DAR&E)

Doberman Assistance, Rescue, and Education, Inc. (DAR&E) is a 501(c)3 non-profit serving Maryland, Washington DC, Virginia, and parts of West Virginia. This volunteer-run organization seeks to provide veterinary care and foster homes for rescued Dobermans and to eventually place these dogs into forever homes. DAR&E prioritizes Dobermans from animal shelters due to the risk of euthanasia but also accepts owner surrenders. More information about DAR&E, including how to volunteer or adopt a Doberman, can be found at their website: www.dobe.net.

The most important quality to look for in a breeder is someone who is willing to help you find the ideal dog for your lifestyle. A good breeder will interview you prior to agreeing to any sale or adoption. They want to make sure their puppies and adult dogs are going to the right homes, so they're willing to spend the extra time ensuring it's a good match. Beware any breeder that tries to talk you into buying a puppy without asking questions about your household and lifestyle. Reputable breeders do not need to convince anyone to take their puppies and, instead, often have long waiting lists for future litters.

Contracts and Guarantees

When you purchase a purebred Doberman Pinscher from a breeder, it's almost guaranteed that the breeder will require you to sign a contract prior to taking the dog home. Contracts are intended to protect both you and the breeder while making sure the puppy's wellbeing is prioritized. The contract will specify which individual dog you're taking home and how much you agreed to pay, as well as any conditions of the purchase or breeder's guarantees.

As the owner, your signature on the contract implies that you are agreeing to take on the responsibility of the puppy's or adult dog's health and wellbeing. Many breeders' contracts include clauses about regular examinations, immunizations, and spaying or neutering when appropriate. If adopted into a pet home rather than a show home, most breeders will require their dogs to be spayed or neutered. If the dog is destined for the show ring, the contract may be different as dogs must be intact to compete in conformation. Some breeders may also return a portion of the original purchase price upon proof of spaying or neutering.

Depending on the breeder's preference, he or she may also state what type of food they want you to feed your new Doberman. Most breeders have owned dogs long enough to know what works best for their animals. This is especially true for breeders that are dedicated raw feeders. Most breeders who raise their puppies on a raw diet will prefer that they go to homes that will continue feeding them a biologically appropriate diet.

There will also be a section of the contract describing the breeder's obligations. They will often guarantee that the puppy is free from genetic diseases or disorders that are common to the Doberman Pinscher. Since a reputable breeder will have tested their dogs prior to breeding, the risk is low, but it's still important to state in the contract. Should a puppy test positive or be diagnosed with the conditions, the contract will also describe what actions will be taken by the breeder and owner. The breeder should be willing to take the dog back, though some owners will have fallen in love enough to keep the puppy regardless of any problems. If a puppy dies from a disease or illness contracted while in the care of the breeder, the contract may also guarantee either a refund or a replacement puppy.

Reputable breeders will also have a clause in their contract stating that if the new owner is no longer able to care for the dog, for any reason, the breeder will take the dog back with no questions asked. Whether the dog needs to be given up due to behavioral problems or a change in the owner's lifestyle, most breeders will gladly take a dog back at any time to prevent the dog from ending up in a shelter or inappropriate home. This rule applies for the entirety of the dog's life.

It's essential that you thoroughly read the contract and discuss it with the breeder prior to signing it. Remember, this is a legally binding document that exists to protect you and the breeder, so if you have any questions or concerns, they need to be addressed before you pick up a pen. Most breeders are happy to explain their contracts to make sure you understand what you are agreeing to before you commit to purchasing a Doberman Pinscher from them.

Health Tests and Certifications

"When choosing a breeder make sure that the breeder does all needed health testing for example vWD, Echo, Holter, Liver Panel, Kidney Panel, Thyroid Panel, OFA Hips, etc. You shouldn't just be buying a dog from a breeder; the breeder should become a friend, mentor and someone you can go to with any questions."

SHARON DUVAL
Kettle Cove Dobermans

All reputable breeders will health test their Doberman Pinschers for common genetic disorders before breeding them. They do this to better the breed as a whole and to eliminate painful disorders from the breed's gene pool. If a single dog in the breeder's program does not pass a test with a satisfactory result, a reputable breeder will spay or neuter the dog rather than risk passing a potential problem on to future generations.

The Orthopedic Foundation for Animals (OFA) is one of the leaders in canine genetic research. The OFA has an online database that contains the test results of individual dogs of nearly every recognized breed. Breeders and owners alike can ask their local veterinarian to perform various health tests and submit the results to the OFA for evaluation for a nominal fee. On the OFA's website, there is a list of recommended tests based on common disorders for each breed. For many tests, the dog is required to be a certain age, usually 12 to 18 months of age, but some tests may not be performed until the dog is at least two years old. Once all tests are performed and submitted to the OFA, the results are recorded in the Canine Health Information Center (CHIC), and each dog is given a CHIC number. The results are made publicly available on the OFA's website and can be found by searching the dog's registered name or CHIC number. If you have any questions about the health testing of a breeder's dogs, you can easily search for the results to verify the information given to you by the breeder.

The OFA requires that results for a series of six tests be submitted for the Doberman breed before a CHIC number can be assigned to an individual dog. The required tests are:

- X-rays for hip dysplasia
- Congenital cardiac exam performed by a board-certified veterinary cardiologist
- Autoimmune thyroiditis evaluation from an OFA approved laboratory
- DNA-based test for von Willebrand's disease
- Working aptitude test issued by the Doberman Pinscher Club of America
- Eye examination performed by a board-certified veterinary ophthalmologist

Remember, a reputable breeder will not be shy about sharing the results of their health testing with you. If a breeder does not provide you with these results, or you cannot find them in the CHIC database, find a different breeder who will be more upfront with you.

Adopting an Adult Dog

Though there are many benefits to bringing home an adult Doberman Pinscher, it's important to realize that there will be bumps in the road. No matter how well behaved your new companion is, he will still experience a stressful transition into your home during the first few weeks. Whether he had lived with a single family his entire life or has been passed from home to home, living with a new family will be stressful. It's crucial that you and your family members understand this and try to be as patient as possible with your new Doberman. It's possible that he may lapse in his housetraining or be a bit shy toward his new family. Patience and under-standing are essential in helping your new Doberman Pinscher through this difficult transition.

When bringing home an adult Doberman Pinscher, you need to realize that your new dog may have already developed certain habits or prefer-ences in his previous homes. It's important to discuss your new dog's prior experiences with the breeder or shelter staff as this may impact whether he will tolerate children or other pets in your home. If you have children or other pets at home, it's important to introduce your new Doberman Pinscher to all human and animal family members prior to bringing him home for the first time. Even if the breeder or shelter volunteers say the dog is fine with kids and other animals, it's best to introduce everyone first to be sure. Always introduce pets on neutral territory to ensure that neither will feel the need to defend their turf from the other. Safely intro-ducing your Doberman Pinscher to your family will be discussed in detail in the next chapter.

How to Choose Your Ideal Dog

"It is important to determine the drive of the specific Doberman you are looking at and if that drive is something you can handle. There are a range drive levels within the breed and they can range from very easy going with mild protection drive to very high drive, which the average home would not be able to handle."

DENISE MORMAN
DeMor Dobermans

Though it can seem daunting to choose your ideal Doberman Pinscher, be sure to seek the advice of the breeder or rescue staff member. If you've already discussed your goals and ideals, as well as any health or behavioral dealbreakers, the breeder or shelter representative will be able to work with you to match you to the perfect dog.

When choosing the perfect Doberman Pinscher, do not focus on appearance. It's easy to fall in love with the sleek and noble appearance of the breed, but just because you find a dog's appearance to be impressive doesn't mean he's the right dog for you and your family. Though you may have a preference in color or general appearance, keep an open mind. A

Photo Courtesy
of Chrissy Mc Falls

dog's temperament should be your priority. If you're looking for a dog to compete with, you'll need to make sure he doesn't have any disqualifying features and possesses the right personality for the show ring or sport of your choice.

Remember, the breeder will know his or her dogs better than anyone, so if you're unsure about which dog is right, be sure to ask for the breeder's opinion. The breeder will be an invaluable resource in matching you to the right dog, so don't disregard their advice even if the dog doesn't look like what you originally had in mind.

CHAPTER 4

Preparing Your Family for a Doberman Pinscher

Yearly Costs of Owning a Doberman Pinscher

Regardless of your income, it's important to understand the financial responsibility of adopting a Doberman Pinscher. The yearly cost of dog ownership is often much more than most people would expect. If you're living on a tight budget, you may need to reconsider bringing a Doberman into your household until you're more financially stable. However, dog ownership is possible for most families with proper preparation and planning.

The initial cost of Doberman Pinscher ownership that you'll encounter is the adoption fee or purchase price. Adopting a dog from a shelter or rescue organization is typically less expensive than buying one from a breeder, but you should still expect to pay anywhere from $50 to $500 or more. The exact cost of the adoption fee will depend on the area you live in and the organization you're adopting from. Most rescue dogs will have been spayed or neutered and

Photo Courtesy of Chrissy Mc Falls

fully vaccinated prior to going to their forever home, so your fee will generally go toward covering the costs of your dog's care during his time at the rescue.

If you're purchasing your Doberman Pinscher from a reputable breeder, you can expect to pay much more than you would at a shelter. While the average price for a pet-quality Doberman Pinscher is about $1,500, prices for show- or sport-quality dogs can be upwards of $3,000. It's not uncommon for adult working Doberman Pinschers to sell for $8,000 or more. Additionally, puppies purchased from breeders will usually only have one round of vaccines and deworming, but adults will have more, so you'll need to account for the cost of initial vet care. You'll also be financially responsible for spaying and neutering your new Doberman Pinscher.

Though the initial cost of your Doberman Pinscher may be the highest cost you deal with, you'll still need to budget for supplies and routine veterinary care. If you already have other dogs, you may not need to buy many new supplies. However, costs can still add up quickly and may vary according to where you live and the quality of food and supplies you buy for your new dog. Excluding the purchase price or adoption fee, you should expect to pay somewhere between $1,065 and $3,810 or more during your first year with your Doberman Pinscher.

Here is a breakdown of the potential costs you may face in the first year of Doberman Pinscher ownership:

Mandatory Expenses	Cost Estimate
Food	$300 - $900
Food and Water Dishes	$10 - $50
Treats	$50 - $150
Toys	$20 - $100
Collars and Leashes	$10 - $100
Crate	$50 - $200
Dog Beds	$50 - $350
Vaccines and Routine Veterinary Care	$150 - $500
Heartworm Testing	$10 - $35
Heartworm Prevention	$25 - $125
Flea and Tick Prevention	$40 - $200
Spaying and Neutering	$150 - $600
Puppy Classes	$200 - $500
Total	**$1,065 - $3,810**

HELPFUL TIP
Homeowner's
Insurance Hikes

Some home insurance companies consider your dog's breed when calculating coverage costs. Regardless of a particular dog's behavior, certain breeds (sometimes including Doberman Pinschers) are considered high risk and can result in higher premiums or denial of home insurance coverage. According to the Insurance Information Institute (III) $675 million was paid by homeowner insurers in liability claims relating to dog bites or dog-related injuries. Laws regarding dog bites and liability vary from state to state.

It's important to recognize that these are not the only costs you'll need to consider during your first year. Doberman Pinschers are quite low maintenance in terms of grooming, but they are large dogs, and not everyone is willing or able to bathe and groom their Doberman at home. Grooming prices vary, but you should expect to pay between $40 and $75 for each grooming appointment.

If you travel frequently, you'll also need to decide whether you want to take your Doberman Pinscher with you or if you'll need to pay for a pet sitter or boarding facility to take care of him in your absence. This cost will also vary according to the area you live in and the quality of care, but you should typically expect to pay upwards of $50 per day.

The highest potential cost that you face as a Doberman Pinscher owner is emergency veterinary care. As your dog's caretaker, you can do your best to keep him safe and healthy, but accidents and illnesses may still occur, so you need to be prepared. Emergency veterinary services can range from a few hundred dollars to several thousand dollars. Surgeries and hospitalizations can be especially costly. Pet insurance is always an option, but this is an additional monthly fee to consider. Many owners, instead, choose to set aside a certain amount of money each month to have on hand in case an emergency should occur. If you're interested in learning more about pet insurance, it will be discussed in detail in Chapter 17.

Possible Expenses	Cost Estimate
Professional Grooming	$100 - $500+
Emergency Veterinary Services	$200 - $2,000+
Pet Sitting or Boarding	$15 - $80+ per day

Though these financial estimates can seem intimidating, this section is not meant to discourage you from Doberman Pinscher ownership. It's simply intended to prepare you for the potential financial burden of bring-ing a dog into your home. Caring for an animal is a huge responsibility that should not be taken lightly, so you may need to plan and budget carefully in order to provide your new Doberman with the best care that you can afford.

Preparing Children

"If there are children in the home, it is your responsibility to monitor your children and teach them how to gently handle the puppy. It will be important to instill good animal handling manners in your children and teach them that the puppy should never be picked up and dropped, they cannot ride on him or pull his ears. Establishing these boundaries with your children as soon as the puppy ar-rives will make a wonderful companion for them as they grow up together."

TRACY DOTY
Halo Dobermans

Photo Courtesy
of Jamie Adkins

Before bringing your Doberman Pinscher home for the first time, you'll need to sit down with your children and discuss the new addition with them. Though it's tempting to surprise your kids with a new puppy, it will be less stressful and overwhelming for both the kids and the puppy if they are prepared beforehand. In the moment, emotions will be elevated, and they may get too excited and frighten the puppy. Scared dogs can and do lash out when they feel the need to protect themselves, so it's best to talk to your children ahead of time about how to interact with the new dog when they first meet him.

Regardless of whether you're bringing home a puppy or an adult Doberman Pinscher, you'll want to explain to your kids that they need to remain calm around the new dog. Ask them to sit or stand quietly and allow their new companion to approach them. Allowing the dog to sniff them before reaching out to pet them is always the safest way to interact for the first time. With puppies, it may be easier for everyone if the kids sit down on the floor so they don't tower over a possibly nervous puppy. The most important rule that you need to explain to your children is that they are never to pick up the puppy. Even a short fall from a child's arms can cause serious injuries, so encourage kids to sit on the floor whenever they want to hold the puppy in their arms.

If your children are old enough to help care for the new Doberman Pinscher, this can be a great opportunity to discuss their responsibilities. You can assign them certain chores, such as feeding or cleaning up after the new dog, if your kids are ready to handle such tasks. It can be incredibly empowering to give children a little responsibility in caring for an animal, so let them help if they are able, but don't forget to supervise when necessary.

Before you bring your Doberman Pinscher home, discuss the rules of the house with your children. For example, if you intend to keep the new dog off the furniture or would prefer him to eat in a specific area of the kitchen, now is the time to talk about it. By explaining the rules beforehand, your family will be able to enforce the rules consistently from the moment your Doberman arrives in his new home.

The Importance of Mutual Respect

As you make plans to bring your Doberman Pinscher home for the first time, it's important to consider the impact this will have on all family members, animal and human. It's crucial for everyone to maintain a certain level of mutual respect during this stressful time. You'll need to work hard to make sure everyone is as comfortable as possible, but there may be bumps in the road regardless. If you have children or other pets in your home, you'll need to make sure you monitor all interactions to ensure that personal boundaries are being respected. It's easy for both kids and dogs to become overstimulated during a play session and act inappropriately, but you can prevent this with proper supervision.

Photo Courtesy of Janessa Cardona

In addition to making sure the new dog feels comfortable, you'll need to make sure that your kids and other pets also feel that their boundaries are being respected. Some pets, especially those that have been alone for a long time, may be unhappy about a new dog in the home. You can help ensure their comfort by providing them with their own safe spaces. Keeping your Doberman Pinscher in a playpen, designated room, or kennel when he's not being supervised can help current pets feel comfortable. This will also keep him out of the kids' toys and belongings, which may cause upset if they are chewed or destroyed. Remember, this is a stressful time for everyone in the family, even if it is exciting, so it's crucial to do what you can to ease your family through this transition.

Playtime with Your Doberman Pinscher

Although playtime can be a great way to bond with your new Doberman Pinscher, it can also lead to problems if you don't encourage your new dog to play appropriately. Rough play can lead to humans and other pets getting knocked over or possibly injured. Many puppies, especially those that are teething, tend to bite during play, so you'll need to actively discourage your Doberman from nipping when he gets excited. Rough play can also escalate into a fight between dogs if one suddenly decides he doesn't like the game anymore. If your Doberman Pinscher tries to engage in rough play, you should discourage it as soon as possible.

Though Dobermans are intelligent dogs that are capable of learning the word 'no' quickly, they may be too wrapped up in a game to listen, so you may need to resort to other methods of discouragement. A spray bottle filled with water can be used to spritz a naughty Doberman and encourage him to listen to his owner. Water is harmless, but it's an unpleasant and distracting sensation, especially when the dog is spritzed in the face. If the play session is with your children, rather than other dogs, you may need to remind your kids to play gently with the new puppy and walk away if it gets too rough.

Many Doberman Pinschers enjoy playing with toys, but there is no single type of toy that appeals to all dogs, so you may need to experiment to see what kind your new companion enjoys. Perhaps he'd enjoy a nice chew or squeaky toy or something sturdy for a game of tug. Some dogs may also enjoy playing fetch with a ball or Frisbee. When buying toys for your new Doberman Pinscher, it's almost guaranteed that he'll be uninterested in some, no matter how much you thought he'd love them, preferring instead to run around with an old sock. Some Dobermans may show no interest in toys at all, preferring instead to chase friends and family around or engage in a wrestling match. The more time you spend with your Doberman Pinscher, the better you'll get to know him and what type of play he enjoys.

Preparing Your Other Pets

Before your Doberman Pinscher comes home for the first time, you'll need to decide how you plan on introducing him to your other pets. This is an especially important event if you're bringing home an adult dog who may have already formed his opinions on other animals. If you have particularly dominant dogs at home, you may want to be cautious about how they'll react to a new companion, especially if your Doberman also has a dominant personality. If you're certain that your current pets will get along with a new dog, consider introducing them on neutral territory outside your home. This will help ensure the success of your introductions, as neither animal will feel the need to defend his property. If you're adopting a Doberman from a shelter or rescue organization, you may be able to perform introductions at the facility or foster home. If you're buying a dog from a breeder, you may be able to bring your other pet along to introduce to your new dog at the breeder's home or somewhere nearby.

Some Doberman Pinschers have a rather strong prey drive, so you'll need to be cautious when introducing your new family member to smaller pets. If your small dog, cat, or other pet becomes fearful, it could trigger your Doberman's prey drive, so it's crucial that you monitor all interactions until you're certain that the animals can be trusted together. Some Dobermans just need a little guidance to let them know how to interact with other animals. However, it's important that you accept that some dogs can never be trusted around small animals and will always need to be separated from them. It's perfectly acceptable to own both a Doberman Pinscher and a pet rabbit and never have them interact if that's the safest option.

It's also possible that your current pets may not get along with your new Doberman Pinscher at first. If this is the case, you'll need to be patient, as many pets can be stubborn in accepting change. This is especially true for older pets, and you may need to go slow with introductions and avoid rushing them into a relationship. You may need to keep them separate until they're ready to spend supervised time together to prevent accidents or injuries from occurring. For more information on introducing your Doberman Pinscher into a multi-pet household, see Chapter 11.

Family Commitment

"The Doberman is a breed that is very devoted to their family and needs to be included in activities. They do not do well being left alone for long periods of time. Those with an active lifestyle who want a great companion for adventures are the best suited for this breed."

ELAINE HOPPER
Starlaine Dobermans

Photo Courtesy
of Jordan Freeborn

Adopting a new dog is a huge commitment, so you need to make sure that everyone in your family is in agreement before you commit to bringing a Doberman Pinscher home. If certain members of your family disagree with this decision, you may need to reconsider or take time to discuss the situation in depth. If everyone does agree with the decision to bring home a new dog, you'll also need to make sure that everyone knows their role in caring for him.

Many owners choose to hold a family meeting prior to making any decisions regarding a new dog. During this discussion, you can make sure that everyone agrees to the adoption and what type of dog they'd like to have in the family. Have each family member make a list of the desired characteristics in their new dog or their desired roles in his care and take these suggestions into consideration when choosing your ideal dog. You may also ask each family member if they have any concerns about the situation, so you can address them before you bring the new dog home. Remember, every member of the family needs to be on the same page in order to make your Doberman Pinscher's arrival go as smoothly as possible.

CHAPTER 5

Preparing Your Home for Your New Doberman Pinscher

Creating a Safe Area Indoors

I t's important to create a safe and comfortable space for your Doberman Pinscher before you bring him home for the first time. Even if you have other pets and your home has been pet-proofed for them, you'll still need to spend some time preparing for the new arrival. Puppies are curious creatures, and it's crucial that you set up a space where your new family member can stay out of trouble. This space will also give your Doberman a comfortable area to retreat to should he feel overwhelmed by new experiences or if you're unable to supervise him.

It's common for new dog owners to set up their new puppy's or adult dog's secure space in a laundry room, bathroom, or section of the kitchen. Smaller rooms or spaces are best for puppies and adults that have not been housetrained. Few dogs will choose to relieve themselves too closely to their eating and sleeping areas if they don't have to, so smaller spaces are ideal for quick housetraining progress. It's also best to choose a space with easy to clean floors, such as those with tile, linoleum, or laminate. You're guaranteed to have at least a few messes, so avoid carpeted areas if possible. You may also want to choose a space that's out of the way of everyday family traffic but isn't secluded enough to make your new Doberman feel isolated. You want him to feel like he's part of the family, but he won't be underfoot all the time.

FUN FACT
Gallant Hearts Puppy Raisers

Doberman Pinschers can make excellent service dogs, though they are more often seen as guard dogs. Gallant Hearts Guide Dog Center, a nonprofit in Madison, MS, has recognized the potential of Doberman Pinschers in a guide-dog capacity and aims to provide well-trained dogs to people who are blind. Gallant Hearts relies on volunteers to raise Boxer, German Shepherd, Golden Retriever, and Doberman Pinscher puppies until they are old enough to become guide dogs.

Photo Courtesy
of Kristi Justiniano

The most important part of deciding where to set up your new Doberman's space is finding an area that can be made secure. Doberman Pinschers are incredibly intelligent dogs that can easily figure out how to escape an area if the opportunity is available. You'll need to make sure your new dog can't jump or push over any barriers. Flimsy baby gates or those that stand freely may need to be avoided until your Doberman is trained well enough to respect such barriers. For most puppies, a sturdy pressure-mounted baby gate should be enough to contain them, at least until they're big enough to jump over it. Playpens and crates are also ideal for keeping your new companion safe and secure. However you choose to contain your Doberman, make sure it's set up or installed properly to prevent escape, potential injury, or damage to your home or personal belongings.

Creating a Safe Outdoor Space

If you have a yard, garden, or other outdoor space, you'll also want to make sure it's a safe and secure space for your Doberman. Some owners choose to set up an area in their yard as a dedicated space for their dogs. You might consider fencing off a certain area of your yard or installing a chain-link or metal bar kennel or dog run.

If you plan on leaving your Doberman Pinscher outdoors for any extended period of time, it's important to make sure that he has everything he needs to stay safe and comfortable. You'll want to provide him with some sort of shelter from the rain and sun. A doghouse or covered area will provide him with the protection he needs to stay cool and dry. Fresh, clean water must be provided at all times, so make sure your dog has enough water and cannot accidentally knock it over. Attaching bowls or buckets to fencing or kennel walls can help ensure that your dog doesn't accidentally spill his water should he get excited. Finally, you'll also want to make sure that your dog has somewhere comfortable to rest. An elevated dog bed is a great option as it will keep your dog off the hard ground and will be easy to clean when needed.

Make sure your Doberman cannot jump or knock over the fencing or barriers around the area. Check for any holes, loose boards, or other ways that your dog may be able to escape. If your adult Doberman discovers that he can climb over the fence, you may need to invest in a kennel with a covered top to prevent him from climbing out. Make sure that all gates or kennel doors latch securely and cannot be undone by the dog from the inside.

You'll also need to consider when it's appropriate for your dog to spend time in his outdoor space. Dobermans are affectionate dogs that love spending time with their family, so if you plan on keeping your Doberman outdoors for extended periods of time, you may want to reconsider getting a dog at all. It's also important to remember that Dobermans do not have the heavy coats needed to stay warm during frigid weather. If your area experiences extreme temperatures, either hot or cold, it's best to keep your dog indoors.

Additionally, if you have other dogs, you'll need to make sure that your new Doberman Pinscher gets along with them prior to leaving them unsupervised in any outdoor space. Accidents can happen in the blink of an eye, especially when dogs are unfamiliar with each other. Though many adult dogs are quite forgiving with puppies, some have a low tolerance for puppy shenanigans and may lash out. If this happens when you're not around, your puppy could become seriously injured or killed. Only leave your pets together unsupervised once you are completely certain that they get along and they will be safe.

Puppy-Proofing Your House

"Dobermans are very agile, very curious breeds. A house needs to be puppy proofed prior to bringing home your new puppy. Also many Doberman puppies love to chew on things such as pillows so keep those away from a new Dobie."

SHARON DUVAL
Kettle Cove Dobermans

After you've set up safe and secure indoor and outdoor spaces for your Doberman Pinscher, you'll want to go through your home and thoroughly puppy-proof it. Even if you have other pets in your home, you'll want to look at your home from the perspective of a curious puppy to make sure there are no obvious dangers that he can get into. Ideally, you should go through your house room by room to make sure any potential dangers are removed or placed out of your new dog's reach. Getting down on the floor at your puppy's height can be helpful in seeing dangers that you might otherwise overlook. Although you should never leave your new puppy unsupervised outside of his secure area, it's important to remove any hazards or temptations in order to keep your puppy safe and save you the frustration of dealing with chewed up belongings. After puppy-proofing your home, you'll want to repeat the process in your yard to make sure it's safe for your new arrival.

As you puppy-proof your home, you may want to consider using child-proof locks for your cabinets in rooms such as the kitchen and bathrooms. This is especially true if your cabinets contain harmful cleaning products, pest control chemicals, or trashcans. You should also pick up all electrical cords off the floor and try to remove anything that is plugged into any outlets that the puppy can reach if possible.

As you move on to the living room, you should move hazardous items like television cables and houseplants to places that are beyond your new Doberman's reach. Plastic zip ties are ideal for keeping electrical cords and cables out of reach and have no permanent effect on your furniture or home. If your home contains any particularly valuable or beloved antiques or furniture, you should consider putting them away until your Doberman has finished teething and is old enough to understand the rules of the house. Curtains and other window coverings are also common targets for playful puppies, so try to tie them up out of the way if possible.

In the bedrooms, it's important to clear the room of items on the floor. Laundry, shoes, and children's toys should all be picked up and placed somewhere out of reach. A Doberman can swallow a sock or toy in only a moment, putting him at risk of choking or an intestinal blockage. In these rooms, it's also important to put electrical cords and houseplants out of the way.

Indoor Dangers

Electrical cords are one of the most common indoor dangers facing your Doberman puppy. Most puppies will view electrical cords as an interesting new toy and try to explore them by using their mouth. Though most shocks are not fatal, it could cause serious burns in and around your puppy's mouth. Rather than risk your puppy's health and safety, it's best to pick up all electrical cords and place them out of reach. Cord covers are also

Photo Courtesy of Rachael Vice

an option, but your puppy may still try to play with them, so it's important that you never allow him in those areas without supervision while he's still learning to leave cords alone.

Household chemicals such as cleaning products and pesticides are also a common danger present in most households. Medication and beauty or hygiene products can also be toxic to dogs, so you'll need to make sure that these types of products are kept behind closed doors or out of reach. If you have houseplants, make sure any plant food and fertilizer are kept far away from your new Doberman.

If you keep indoor plants, you'll also need to make sure that they are not toxic to pets, even if you already have pets in the home. Your current pets may have already learned to leave the houseplants alone, but your puppy won't understand that yet. If consumed, toxic plants can cause problems ranging from mild gastrointestinal distress to seizures and even death, so it's important to either remove the toxic plants from the home or place them out of your Doberman's reach. If you're uncertain about which plants in your home may be toxic, the ASPCA's website has a complete list of common houseplants that are poisonous to pets. Even if you discover that your plants are harmless, it's still best to place them where your Doberman can't get to them.

If you're bringing home a puppy or senior dog, you'll also need to be cautious about any stairs. Particularly young and old dogs often do not possess the physical strength and agility needed to safely navigate flights of stairs without assistance, and serious injuries can occur if they should fall. Keeping doors shut or installing pressure-mounted baby gates will help keep your new companion safe without causing your human family members any inconvenience.

One of the most overlooked dangers inside your house is your trashcan. Make sure it is secure and unable to be opened by your dog, or place it behind a closed door or inside a cabinet. Trashcans can contain everything from plastic to broken glass to leftover food. In addition to the dangers of a trashcan's contents, this bad habit is self-rewarding, so make sure that your dog is never given the chance to experience it in the first place. If your home doesn't have a cabinet or closet that will fit the trashcan, there are many on the market designed to lock and keep out even the most persistent pet.

Outdoor Dangers

Your yard or garden may also contain potential dangers, so it's important to thoroughly puppy-proof your outdoor space prior to your new Doberman Pinscher's arrival. One of the biggest dangers is an unsecure fence. You'll want to walk along your fence and closely examine every inch in search of holes, rotten wood, loose boards, and broken latches. You'll also want to make sure that your Doberman will not be able to climb over the fence. An adult Doberman can easily jump over a small fence or climb over one made of chain-link. Should your dog escape, he could fall victim to speeding cars, wild animals, or even unscrupulous human beings.

If you have a pool in your outdoor space, you will also need to make sure its fence is secure as well. Some pool fencing may have gaps big enough for a Doberman puppy to squeeze through, so you may need to line the fence with something like chicken wire to keep your puppy out. If your pool doesn't have

Photo Courtesy
of Deborah Smith

a fence around it, make sure your Doberman is never allowed unsupervised access to the pool area. Even a healthy adult dog can drown if it panics after falling in and becomes disoriented enough that it cannot find the way out.

As with your indoor plants, make sure your outdoor space does not contain plants that are toxic to dogs. If you have a vegetable or flower garden that you would like to protect from your Doberman, consider fencing it off. Even if the plants are not toxic, you may not appreciate your puppy digging up your favorite plants. If you use any type of chemical pesticide or fertilizer, you'll also want to keep your dog away from your plants to prevent him from accidentally ingesting harmful chemicals.

You may also want to limit your Doberman's access to areas such as your garage or shed. Many garages and sheds contain dangers such as pesticides and antifreeze. Antifreeze, in particular, is a common danger, and many pets across the country fall victim to antifreeze poisoning each year. Antifreeze tastes sweet, and many pets find the flavor appealing, so it's important to keep it out of reach and clean up any leaks as soon as possible. When consumed, antifreeze can cause serious kidney damage and even death. No matter how thoroughly you puppy-proof your home and outdoor space, you should consider looking up the number for your local poison control center to keep in a convenient place.

Crates and Crate Training

"Crate training is crucial. The puppy should feel safe. Make it a quiet space and start with a covering to simulate a den. The puppy should go in the crate and if it whines and or cries do not acknowledge that behavior. After several nights they will be just fine and it will be a safe space for them anytime you will need to leave them."

DENISE MORMAN
DeMor Dobermans

Crate training should be an essential part of your Doberman Pinscher's education, regardless of his age. Even if you do not intend to use a crate once he becomes trustworthy enough to have access to your entire home, he'll still need to understand how to rest calmly in a crate or cage when at the vet or groomer.

Dogs that haven't been properly crate trained risk injuring themselves or others if they panic once the door is closed behind them. These dogs usually have to be forced into the crate rather than entering on their own, increasing their panic and making it difficult for veterinary staff members and groomers to do their jobs. Dogs that haven't been crate trained often bark incessantly and dig or chew at the sides and door of the crate. Broken nails and teeth and scraped or cut paws are common injuries incurred in these moments of panic. A lack of crate training not only puts your dog at risk of injury, but it makes him incredibly difficult to handle even by professionals. To prevent stress and injury caused by panic, it's best to teach your dog that crates are a safe place to relax and unwind.

With proper training, your Doberman will come to view his crate as a safe space that he can retreat to when he needs a break from the hustle and bustle of your family's everyday life. For dogs that have been properly trained, crates can become a portable source of comfort, allowing you to keep your dog calm and relaxed wherever you go.

First, you'll need to decide what type of crate you'd like for your Doberman Pinscher. Crates come in a variety of materials, including wood, metal, and plastic. Most wooden crates are more aesthetically pleasing than wire crates, but will not stand up to destructive dogs. Many metal crates, on the other hand, are designed to withstand heavy chewers. Plastic crates, most of which are approved for air travel, are typically quite inexpensive. Metal wire crates are also less costly than crates made of fashionable wood or heavy-duty metal.

Choosing the right size crate for your Doberman is crucial, though it can be more difficult with growing puppies. The crate needs to be large enough for your dog to be able to stand up, turn around, and lie down. However, it

shouldn't be so large as to encourage your dog to use part of the crate as a bathroom. With puppies, you may find yourself changing crate sizes every few months until your dog reaches adulthood. You may also consider using a crate with a movable divider so you can adjust the size of your dog's crate space as needed.

In order to make your Doberman feel at ease with his new crate, you'll want to start by making it as comfortable as possible. You can place his favorite bed, blankets, and toys inside as long as you're confident that he won't destroy them while unsupervised. If you find that your new dog becomes destructive while crated, remove any bedding or toys to prevent him from accidentally or purposefully swallowing any pieces.

Once you've made the crate as appealing as possible, toss a few treats inside to see if your Doberman will enter the crate on his own. At first, he may reach in for the treats and back out immediately, but with practice and plenty of positive reinforcement, he'll begin to spend more time inside. As he becomes more comfortable in the crate, you can try shutting the door behind him. At first, try closing the door for just a second or two before rewarding him. As he progresses, you can leave the door shut for longer periods of time. However, it's important that you do not let your dog out if he begins to bark or whine. If you release him when he's upset, he'll learn that making a ruckus will make you open the door for him. Instead, give him a chance to calm down and release him as soon as he quiets down.

Supplies

Before you bring your Doberman Pinscher home for the first time, make a list of supplies to ensure you have everything you need. If you have other dogs in your home, you may already have the majority of the necessary supplies, but it can still be helpful to make a list to be sure. If your current dogs have trouble sharing, you should consider buying new toys and treats to prevent any problems with resource guarding.

Food – Though food is one of the most important supplies, it can easily be overlooked in the stressful moments before bringing your new family member home. Prior to pick-up, ask your breeder or the shelter staff what type of food your Doberman is currently eating and buy that type of food. If you do not plan on continuing with that type of food, you may only need to buy a small amount. In order to prevent digestive upset, feed your dog that food for a few days before slowly transitioning to the food of your choice. You should also ask about any known food sensitivities, so you can purchase the appropriate food and treats.

Collar and leash – You'll want to have an appropriately sized collar waiting for your new Doberman Pinscher when he arrives home from the breeder or shelter. Many types of collars are adjustable, so you'll be able to estimate the right size if you aren't completely certain. You can find a wide selection of collars at your local pet store or favorite online retailer's website. You'll need to decide what color you'd like, what style, and whether you'd prefer it to be made out of nylon, biothane, or leather. You can choose a collar to match your new companion's personality or represent your favorite sports team. The choice is yours, but don't forget to pick up a matching leash. You should also consider buying an identification tag with your phone number or address on it in case your Doberman manages to escape from his new home.

The best type of collar or harness to buy for your Doberman will depend on your own preferences, your trainer's recommendations, and what you intend to do with your new dog. If you intend to compete in a sport or train your Doberman as a working dog, you may need to invest in sport-specific gear. Your dog's needs will be less specific if you just plan on walking around your neighborhood, but your dog's harness or collar should still fit snugly but comfortably. It should be noted that although there are plenty of tools, including collars, harnesses, and headcollars that are intended to discourage dogs from pulling, the best way to stop your dog from dragging you around is proper training. Teaching your dog to walk on a loose leash will be discussed in detail in Chapter 12. If your dog is prone to slipping out of his collar, you should look for a martingale or limited-slip style collar. These types of collars will become tighter if your dog pulls but will not tighten enough to restrict breathing.

There are collars, harnesses, and leashes that should be avoided by the average dog owner. Training collars such as e-collars and prong collars can be useful tools, but only in the hands of someone experienced in their use. A dog can be seriously injured if training collars are used improperly. If you plan on using a harness with your Doberman, you should avoid harnesses that lay laterally across the chest. Instead, look for a Y-shaped harness that will not restrict your dog's movement or impede his gait. This includes harnesses that require the leash to attach to the front. That style of harness will restrict your dog's movement by constantly pulling his chest to the side when he puts tension on the leash. Over time, restricted movement can cause rubbing, lameness, or injury. Retractable leashes should also be avoided. Though it may be tempting to give your dog more freedom on his daily walks, retractable leashes put your dog and others at risk of injury. These types of leashes do not allow you to retrieve your dog quickly should he get into trouble. Even if you believe your dog is friendly, other dog owners will not want him to approach their dogs without permission as their dogs may not be as sociable. Additionally, if pedestrians or cyclists are present where you walk your dog, you may find yourself and your dog tangled up with a very upset individual.

Dog bed – Though you may want to spoil your new family member, consider purchasing an inexpensive dog bed for him at first. If you're bringing home a young Doberman, he may quickly outgrow an appropriately sized bed or chew it up when teething. Dogs also have different sleeping styles, so regardless of your new dog's age, you may want to find out if he prefers to sleep flat on his side or curled up before buying him a nicer bed in his preferred shape. No matter what type of bed you choose, try to buy one with a removable cover, which makes cleaning up messes a breeze. For older Dobermans, memory foam is a popular option to help ease the aches that come with age.

Toys – Some Doberman Pinschers can be heavy chewers, so you might want to consider purchasing extra-durable dog toys. However, older dogs often prefer softer toys that are easier on the teeth and jaws. You may only want to buy a single toy or two at first as you'll want to get to know your new dog better before filling his toy box. Some dogs will prefer balls over squeaky toys, while others love a good game of Frisbee, so it may take some trial and error to find your new dog's favorite type of toy.

Grooming supplies – Whether you plan on doing all of your Doberman Pinscher's grooming yourself or having a professional take care of it, it can be helpful to have some grooming supplies on hand. The more practice he has with the grooming process in the comfort of his own home, the better behaved he'll be at the salon. A soft bristle brush or deshedding blade can be helpful in removing dead hair and preventing it from being spread all over your home. Shampoos and conditioners are also nice to have on hand in case your dog gets into something smelly between regular trips to the groomer. If you plan on trimming your Doberman's nails yourself, you'll also need to purchase a nail clipper or grinder. The grooming supply section of your local pet store can be overwhelming if you're not sure what you need, so be sure to ask your groomer for advice on which products are best for your dog's coat. Basic grooming will be discussed more in Chapter 16.

Housetraining supplies – No matter what age your new Doberman is, it's a good idea to include housetraining supplies on your pet store shopping list. Even if your new dog has already been housetrained, the stress of moving into a new home can cause even the most well-behaved dogs to experience a lapse in training. As always, it's better to be prepared and have the necessary cleaning supplies at the ready. Disposable or reusable puppy pads are also a great option, especially for puppies.

There is a variety of cleaning products on the market that contain enzymes to help eliminate odors and stains. Some owners may also choose to invest in a set of housetraining bells to be hung on the door. You can teach your Doberman to nudge the bells with his paw or nose to let you know when he's ready to go outside. However, the most essential housetraining item you need to include on your list is an appropriately sized crate. If you have it ready to go before you bring your new family member home, you can begin crate training immediately.

Basic Shopping List for Your New Doberman Pinscher

- Collar and leash
- Identification tag
- Crate
- Bedding
- Food and water bowls
- Treats
- Toys
- Combs or brushes
- Shampoo
- Nail trimmer
- Puppy pads
- Cleaning supplies

CHAPTER 6
Bringing Your New Doberman Pinscher Home

The Importance of Having a Plan

I deally, your first day at home with your Doberman Pinscher should be as stress free as possible for you, your new dog, and your current family members. Though you won't be able to eliminate all stress during the first few days together, bringing a new dog into an unprepared home is not recommended. Instead, set yourself up for success by developing a plan for your new dog from the moment you pick him up from the breeder or shelter.

First, you'll need to prepare a set of household rules for your new Doberman Pinscher. If you currently have other pets in your home, you may already have an idea of what boundaries to set for your new companion. However, if your new dog will be the only furry member of the family, you'll need to decide what behaviors you will and won't allow. For example, do you plan on allowing your new dog on the furniture? Where will he sleep for the first few weeks? You'll need to discuss these rules with all human members of your family to make sure that everyone is on the same page.

It can be helpful for some families to write down the rules of the house, especially if some members are prone to forgetfulness or would prefer a visual representation of the new dog's boundaries. If your family members have varying schedules, do your best to accommodate your dog's preferred schedule. Consistency won't always be possible, but you should aim to be as consistent as you can. Again, you won't be able to eliminate all stressors from your first few days with your new Doberman Pinscher, but thorough preparation can help everything go more smoothly.

Photo Courtesy of Kaitlin Witmer

Developing a Schedule

During your early discussions about your new Doberman Pinscher, consider talking to your family about what an average day will look like once your new dog has arrived. It can be stressful to welcome a new dog into your home, but a regular schedule can help both you and the dog adjust more quickly. Just remember that a puppy will not be able to go more than a few hours between bathroom breaks, so you'll need to either be flexible with your schedule or coordinate with other family members to make sure your new dog can go outside when he needs to. You'll also need to plan for consistent mealtimes and regular walks.

For some families, writing down a weekly schedule and deciding in advance who will be responsible for your new Doberman throughout the day can be helpful in making sure everyone's needs are being met. Young children can help out with the regular care of their new pet with proper supervision. Older

Photo Courtesy
of Sofia Edholm

children may be allowed more responsibility, but it's up to you to determine if your kids are ready for additional duties. You might even consider assigning each family member a certain task or day of the week that they will be responsible for in order to make sure it's done properly. If you don't establish clear communication with your family regarding your dog's schedule, it's possible for him to be served two breakfasts or have his morning walk forgotten. While situations like that won't harm your Doberman, they will make it more difficult

DOBERMANS IN FICTION
Swindle Series

Gordon Korman, a Canadian American author of over 80 books for children and young adults, is the author of the eight-book Swindle series. This beloved series follows a band of kids as they go on a myriad of adventures and heists. Featured in the series is a Doberman named Luthor, a dog who both hinders and helps the team throughout the series and has a central role in many of the books.

for him to adjust to his new home. The more consistency you can provide, the better he'll begin to understand the rules of your home.

Picking Your Dog Up from the Breeder or Shelter

If you've thoroughly prepared your home and your family for the new arrival, picking your Doberman Pinscher up from the breeder or shelter should be a relatively low-key event. The day before you bring your new dog home, double-check your preparations, and make sure that you have everything you need. If you need to pick up any last-minute supplies, do so before you bring your Doberman home. You might also consider going through each area of your home one more time to make sure it has been thoroughly puppy-proofed.

Most breeders and shelters require you to sign their contract or adoption agreement prior to allowing the dog to go home, so if you've already done so, take a moment to review the document once more. Make sure you agree to everything and that the information is accurate. If you've already paid an adoption fee or placed a deposit on the puppy, make sure that amount is mentioned in the contract and that you're aware of any balance you may still owe. Remember, the contract or adoption agreement is a legally binding document, so it's crucial that the information it contains is accurate and you agree to each and every requirement. If you do still owe a portion of the purchase price or adoption fee, don't forget to bring enough cash or a check to cover the balance.

If you have any last-minute questions about the puppy, the Doberman breed, or anything else, it can be helpful to write them down before going to pick up your new family member. This way, you'll be able to remember your questions even if you're a bit overwhelmed by your new dog. However, if you don't have any questions or forget to ask, most breeders and shelters are happy to stay in contact afterward to make the transition as smooth as possible. In fact, most reputable breeders are happy to stay in touch for your dog's entire life. They are usually happy to answer any questions that may arise and enjoy seeing how their puppies grow and develop in their new homes.

The Ride Home

Many new dog owners put little thought into the ride home, but it can be an incredibly frightening experience for a puppy who has never been without his mother and siblings. It's likely that he has had little experience riding in cars and he will be surrounded by new people, so nervousness should be expected. Since you want your Doberman Pinscher to be a confident traveler, you'll want to make it a positive experience. Just remember to stay calm, no matter how the dog reacts. Though you may be excited about your new family member coming home, excitement will only escalate his fear. These same concepts apply not only to puppies but to adult dogs as well. Unless you know the complete history of your new adult Doberman, it's difficult to determine how much experience he has had with traveling or if those experiences were positive. The best approach is to treat the ride home like it's your new dog's first time in a car.

The most important aspect of the ride home is safe restraint. Though you may be tempted to ride with your new puppy in your lap, it's a safer choice for everyone in the vehicle to keep him properly restrained. There are many different methods of safe restraint, depending on your dog's size and travel experience. Most dogs are quite comfortable riding in a crate as it gives them a sense of comfort to be in a den-like space. You may also consider bringing home a small blanket or toy with the scent of the puppy's mother and littermates for comfort. If your dog is a more experienced traveler, or your car isn't large enough for a crate that will comfortably hold your new Doberman, you may also consider a doggy seatbelt. Most doggy seatbelts allow the dog to wear a harness with a short leash that either wraps around the headrest or clips into the seatbelt buckle. Another option is using a metal or fabric barrier to keep your dog in the back seat or cargo area. Properly restraining your new Doberman will not only keep you and your family safe but other drivers on the road as well.

Motion sickness is a common experience with dogs who haven't traveled much, but even experienced travelers can become sick from time to time, so you should be prepared. Consider carrying disposable or reusable puppy pads, towels, or blankets in the car just in case. You can line your dog's crate or the backseat or cargo area of your car to aid in cleanup. You may also want to consider investing in a waterproof seat protector or cargo area cover. It can also be helpful to bring along a plastic bag or container to store any soiled linens until you're able to wash them.

It's possible that your Doberman may react with extreme fear, especially if it's his first time in a car. Some dogs may just shake nervously while remaining relatively quiet, but it's also possible that your new dog may panic

Photo Courtesy of Collin and Kayla Williams

or try to escape. This is why you want your dog to be safely restrained. If he panics and leaps into your lap as you're driving down the freeway, an accident can occur. Remember, no matter how frightened your dog is, it's crucial that you remain calm. Even if you are anxious, you must set an example to show that you are the calm, confident leader he needs you to be.

The First Night Home

"It is important to let your puppy cry a while for the first night. He will soon tire, settle down and drift off to sleep. It is extremely important to be patient with your puppy the first few days and give him time to warm up to his new family. You must remember he was uprooted from everything familiar to him and will need some time to adjust."

TRACY DOTY
Halo Dobermans

Ideally, you should bring your Doberman Pinscher home on a weekend or the night before your day off. Your first night home with your new family member is unlikely to be very restful, so it's best if you don't have any early appointments or responsibilities the following morning. Even if you're bringing home an adult dog rather than a puppy, your new companion may still be restless during his first night in his new home. This is an especially stressful time for puppies, as it may be their first night away from their mother and littermates.

Though you may be tempted to put your yapping puppy to bed in a room that's out of earshot, you'll only increase his fear and anxiety by isolating him. If possible, you should keep him in a crate or playpen next to your bed. Allowing a new, possibly unhousetrained dog to sleep in your bed or have free rein over your house isn't recommended. Instead, keep him in a small area where he'll be able to see and smell you.

The first night home will be your first chance to develop your nightly routine. Make sure you take the dog out as close to bedtime as possible. If you've brought home a Doberman puppy, you'll probably be waking up every few hours to take him outside, so taking him out just before bed will allow you to get at least a couple hours of sleep before the next bathroom break. Most experts recommend allowing your puppy to hold his bladder for one hour for every month of his age. So, if you're bringing home a two-month-old puppy, you'll need to take him outside every two hours or risk cleaning up a mess. Though adults may technically be able to hold it all night, if your new adult

Photo Courtesy
of Kristina and Marco DelPriore

Doberman isn't housetrained or you aren't sure, you may want to take him out periodically throughout the night until you're confident in his housetraining.

It's almost guaranteed that your new dog is going to cry during the night, but it's up to you to determine whether those cries are a request to go outside or just a demand for attention. If your Doberman has had a recent bathroom break, you can assume that he just wants attention. If it has been some time since his last trip outside, it may be time for a break.

If you believe your dog is only crying for attention, it's important to ignore him. Though it may be difficult to ignore loud barks, whines, and howls, responding will only encourage this type of behavior. Instead, wait for him to settle down. Note the frequency of your dog's bathroom breaks during this first night. That will be helpful in developing a regular nighttime schedule that you'll be able to stick to during the following weeks and months with your new Doberman Pinscher.

CHAPTER 7
The First Few Weeks

"Be prepared for a very smart dog that will want to be in charge of you. If you do not teach them, they will teach you."

DENISE MORMAN
DeMor Dobermans

Standing by Your Expectations

During the first few weeks at home with your new Doberman Pinscher, it's important to be realistic about your expectations. This can be a challenging time period, and you need to keep your expectations low until your new family member settles into his new home. Whether you've brought home a puppy or an adult, it's important to remember that the more work you put into your new dog's training, the more quickly he's going to adapt to his new home. If you dedicate just 30 minutes per week to your Doberman's education, you're not going to see the same progress that you would if you train in shorter, more frequent sessions. Infrequent training is only going to result in frustration for both you and your new dog, simply because you'll spend the majority of each session going over what you taught him in the last session rather than making any real progress. Over time, this repetition may even make your dog uninterested in future training sessions.

However, you should also avoid spending every moment of your day training your Doberman Pinscher. It's crucial to remember that this may be an unsettling and even frightening time for him, so you need to be especially patient and forgiving during the first few

FUN FACT
Captain Kirk's Dogs

William Shatner, the Canadian actor who famously portrayed Captain James T. Kirk in the *Star Trek* franchise, has owned a number of Dobermans throughout his life. The names of his Dobermans include Morgan, Kirk, China, Heidi, Paris, Royale, Martika, Sterling, Charity, Bella, Starbuck, Espresso, and Macchiato.

*Photo Courtesy
of Amy DeRidder*

weeks. Though he may have learned basic commands or the rules of the house in his previous home, the stress of rehoming can cause him to temporarily forget what he learned or purposely act out. For more sensitive dogs, diving straight into a full-time training program moments after arriving in a new home can be stressful and overwhelming. Instead, allow your Doberman to have an adjustment period and introduce him to the rules of the house or basic commands in short, fun training sessions throughout the day. Even if he only learns a few things in the first few weeks, you can consider your training a success. Remember, consistency is key when it comes to dog training, but keeping your expectations low in the beginning will help to prevent frustration and resentment from developing.

Establishing Household Rules

The first few weeks at home with your Doberman Pinscher will give you the opportunity to establish the rules of your household, as long as you're willing to enforce them consistently. Prior to the arrival of your new dog, you'll need to discuss these rules with members of your household so that you'll be able to address any issues when they arise. It's also important for each member of the family to actively take part in the new dog's training in order to maintain the consistency needed for successful training.

One of the first rules you should teach your Doberman Pinscher is that humans must be allowed to go through doorways before dogs. Not only is it rude for a dog to shove his way through a doorway before a human, but small children and seniors could potentially be injured if they are knocked to the ground in the process. It also puts the dog's safety at risk if he manages to shove his way out your front door alone. Teach your Doberman to wait politely at doorways by asking him to sit or stand patiently each time you open a door. At first, he may get excited and try to get through, especially if the door leads to an outdoor space. However, since he's not allowed to bolt through the doorway, he must sit or stand as calmly as possible while you go through the doorway first. Once you've gone through, you can invite the dog to join you by giving him a release command such as 'OK.' You must be careful not to allow him to come through before he is released, so if he leaves his waiting position prematurely, return him to his original position and try again. Eventually, the dog will understand that he's expected to wait patiently until he's invited.

Moving out of the way when asked is also an essential skill that any dog should possess. Whether you're asking him to get off your favorite chair or leave the kitchen while you cook, your new Doberman needs to move when you ask him to. In a natural pack setting, only the alpha dog is allowed to stay where he is, while more submissive dogs must move around him. By allowing your dog to stay where he is when he's in the way, you're only enforcing the false notion that he's the one in charge. To teach your Doberman Pinscher to move when asked, there are several methods you may choose to use. Some methods work better in different situations, so you'll need to consider which methods will work for you and your dog.

First, you can try keeping a 'drag line' on your dog, which is a short leash designed to be dragged around the house. Drag lines are not long enough to get caught on anything, but they're long enough that you can grab it if you need to. If your dog reacts aggressively to having his collar grabbed, drag lines are a great way to accomplish the same control while keeping your hands safe from your dog's teeth. You can also attempt to lure your dog out of the way with treats. As you lure, give your verbal command of choice so that the Doberman will begin to connect the behavior with the command. You can also try pushing your dog out of the way but use caution as some dogs may also react negatively to this type of pressure. Though results vary, most owners find success using a combination of a drag line and plenty of positive reinforcement.

Photo Courtesy
of Emily Williams

Common Puppy Problems

"Dobermans are independent thinkers and therefore can be a challenge to train. They are very intelligent and require a trainer that is on the ball at all times."

ELAINE HOPPER
Starlaine Dobermans

During the first few weeks or even months, with your Doberman Pinscher puppy, you're bound to encounter a few common problems. Though most of these problems can be easily corrected, consistency is crucial in order to prevent your new family member from developing annoying or harmful bad habits. Preventing bad behaviors from developing in the first place is always easier than correcting them once they're established. Consistency is key, so you will need to focus on proper supervision and puppy management so that you can correct bad behavior immediately. This is especially important with self-rewarding bad behaviors, as you'll need to prevent your puppy from having the opportunities to engage in naughty behavior that he will want to repeat in the future.

One of the most common and obnoxious behaviors you'll face as a puppy owner is chewing. This unavoidable behavior comes naturally to puppies of any age but can intensify during teething, which occurs between the ages of four and six months. As your puppy's adult teeth come in, he may experience pain and discomfort and may resort to chewing in an attempt to soothe his aching gums. During this time, you'll need to be especially observant so as not to give your puppy an opportunity to chew things he shouldn't. Leaving your puppy in the house without supervision is irresponsible, so you will want to place him in a crate or other secure area if you're too busy to keep a close watch on him. You'll also want to discourage him from chewing furniture and personal items by giving him safe alternatives such as chew toys and edible chews.

Digging is also a commonly encountered problem with puppies and can become a problem in both indoor and outdoor spaces. Turning your Doberman loose in your outdoor space without supervision is a sure way to encourage bad habits like digging, as is allowing your dog unsupervised access to your home. Though dogs most often develop digging habits in gardens and yards, you may also see your dog digging at furniture or in potted indoor plants. Not only is digging messy and destructive, but it can also be dangerous if your dog happens to ingest any dirt, rocks, or sticks that he digs up. Digging can also damage your dog's paw pads and nails. Additionally, it's also possible for a dog that digs to escape even the most secure fence by burrowing underneath it. In order to prevent any accidents, injuries, or damage to your home, you need to discourage digging from the very beginning. This is a difficult habit to break once established, so make sure your corrections are consistent.

Excessive barking can also be a common and frustrating habit encountered by new dog owners. Doberman Pinschers are natural guard dogs, so

Photo Courtesy of Susie Garcia

you may want to allow your dog a warning bark or two, but you should discourage any more than is necessary. A bark or two will be enough for your Doberman to fulfill his duties as the protector of his home and family but won't irritate you or your neighbors. Some dogs may resort to excessive barking as a form of entertainment or frustration due to insufficient physical and mental stimulation. As with digging, you need to be sure that you never give your Doberman the opportunity to develop this habit and stay consistent in your corrections.

With both barking and digging, you can discourage these behaviors from the start by distracting your dog with a loud clap, stomp, or 'No.' With repetition, your Doberman will realize that these behaviors only result in an unpleasant sound from you, and he will be less likely to attempt to bark or dig in the future. However, some dogs may be particularly defiant, so you may want to try using a water bottle to correct the behavior. As you give your verbal correction, such as 'no,' you can spray the dog in the face with water. Water won't cause your dog any harm, but most dogs do not enjoy the sensation of getting sprayed in the face, so it's typically an effective correction. Whatever you do, never hit, kick, or yell at your dog to correct his behavior. Your dog will not understand that you are correcting him and will likely react out of fear. As long as you stay consistent in your training, harsh corrections are never necessary.

Leaving Your Dog Home Alone

Though it may be tempting to spend every moment with your new companion, you're going to need to leave the house at some point. In order to minimize the stress on both you and your new Doberman Pinscher, you'll need to do a little preparation before leaving. Preparation and stress management can also help to prevent separation anxiety, which is an incredibly difficult behavior to correct once established.

The most important step in leaving or entering your home is to be as relaxed about it as possible. It can be difficult not to share the excitement of seeing your dog after a long day of work or give a long, drawn-out goodbye, but it's crucial that you refrain and not make a big deal out of your Doberman staying home alone. If he becomes stressed or excited, ignore him until he's calmed down. Once he's mellowed out, give him a calm greeting. If you're leaving, do so calmly without saying goodbye. By not adding to his elevated emotions, you're letting your dog know that the situation is under control, regardless of whether he's home with you or alone.

You want to give your dog the confidence he needs to behave himself in your absence, so start practicing your departure. Go through your normal routine of picking up your keys, putting on your shoes and jacket, and walking through the door. Then, wait outside for a moment or two and go back indoors and act as though you're coming home from work or running errands. With enough repetition, your Doberman will begin to understand that it's not a big deal for you to leave the house or come home. As you practice, increase the amount of time you wait outside. Try taking a walk around the block, checking the mail, or even running a few errands.

If your Doberman Pinscher really seems to struggle with being left home alone, you may want to consider getting him a companion. Remember, dogs are pack animals, and many will do better with a friend to keep them company. Though many dogs prefer the companionship of their own species, some dogs are fine with a cat or other type of pet. Consider your dog's individual personality and preferences when deciding what type of companion would be best. It's important to note that some Dobermans are prone to same-sex aggression and may prefer a companion of the opposite sex. Same-sex aggression will be discussed in detail in Chapter 10.

Training and Puppy Classes

"The Doberman is a very intelligent breed; the owner needs to be on their toes at all times. My first obedience class the trainer was a Doberman breeder, he said to the class (which was mostly Dobermans) 'as the handler/trainer, you need to be smarter than your dog'."

DEE ROBISON
DeeRun Dobermans

If you aren't making as much progress in your Doberman Pinscher's training as you would like in the first few weeks, consider signing up for training classes. If you're inexperienced with dog training, it can be incredibly beneficial to work with a professional to help you and your dog meet your training goals, improve your relationship, and make the transition into Doberman ownership as smooth as possible. Important skills such as sit, down, and stay will help your dog become a well-behaved member of the family, and training classes can help socialize him with new people, places, and dogs.

Most puppy classes require participants to be of a certain age to ensure that all puppies have received the necessary vaccinations to keep everyone in the class safe from illness. Since particularly young puppies do not have strong immune systems, parasites and disease can spread from puppy to puppy quickly. It's likely that the trainer or training facility will require proof of vaccinations and flea and tick prevention before the first day of class.

Photo Courtesy of Jordan Freeborn

If you've adopted an adult Doberman Pinscher, you won't be able to participate in puppy classes, but most trainers and training facilities offer basic obedience classes for dogs of any age to learn the basics. Depending on where you live, you may be able to find classes at formal obedience schools, local pet stores, or even shelters or rescue organizations. Trainers may also be available to give you and your Doberman private lessons in the comfort of your own home or a local training facility or park. Private training sessions are ideal for dogs with socialization issues or behavioral problems. Group classes may also be available and are perfect for dogs needing a bit of socialization without the worry of aggression or reactivity. Private lessons are often more expensive than group lessons, so you'll need to budget accordingly.

Take It Slow

During the first few weeks, you're guaranteed to have a few ups and downs with your new Doberman Pinscher. However, it's important to remain patient no matter how challenging the situation may seem. There may be instances where you feel overwhelmed or frustrated, but there will also be times where you are elated and proud of your new companion. Just remember to keep your expectations low and stay positive and patient. Introducing a new dog into your home can be a stressful experience, so take it slow.

You may be tempted to dive right into training your new Doberman Pinscher. After all, they are a biddable and intelligent breed, but it's crucial to remember that this is a new experience for your dog too. You don't want to cause him any more stress than necessary. Of course, you need to start introducing the rules of the house right away but try to keep training sessions short and sweet. If your new dog seems to struggle with a certain concept, try practicing a more familiar task so that you can reward him for a job well done. You can always return to the challenge at a later date. The more positive reinforcement you use in your training during this initial period, the more engaged and interested your dog will be. He'll also be less likely to lose focus due to stress or frustration.

CHAPTER 8
Health and Wellness

Choosing a Veterinarian

If you have other pets in your home, it's likely that you already have an established relationship with a veterinarian in your area. If not, you'll need to do some research to find a reputable local veterinarian to provide medical care for your new Doberman Pinscher. Though that may seem like a daunting task, there are many ways to find the right veterinarian for your new companion.

Your first resource for a veterinarian recommendation should be the breeder or rescue organization that you got your Doberman from, as long as you didn't travel out of state to pick up your new dog. Both breeders and rescues will have ongoing relationships with a veterinary clinic that they know and trust. Additionally, veterinary staff at the recommended clinics will be familiar with the breed and may have already been providing care to your dog since his first vet visit.

However, if you adopted your Doberman Pinscher from a shelter instead of a breed-specific or foster home-based organization, it may be more difficult for them to provide a vet recommendation as they often use on-site shelter veterinarians or volunteers from several local clinics. You may also be out of luck if you adopted your dog from a breeder or rescue in another state.

If you have friends or family in your area with dogs, they may be able to provide you with a recommendation for a reputable veterinarian. Local dog trainers and groomers are also a great resource, as are local dog shows and training classes. The more dog people you have in your life, the more information you'll be able to get about local veterinary clinics so that you can decide which one may be best for your new family member.

You should also consider what type of veterinary care you'd like for your Doberman Pinscher. Most clinics focus on more traditional veterinary

FUN FACT
All I Want for Christmas

American singer and songwriter Mariah Carey owned two Dobermans named Duke and Princess during the 1990s. Princess starred in Carey's music video for "All I Want for Christmas is You."

*Photo Courtesy
of Heather Rosati*

medicine, so if you would prefer holistic care or alternative therapies, you may need to research your options. A directory of holistic veterinarians can be found on the American Holistic Veterinary Medical Association (AHVMA) website and can be searched according to species and treatment type. If you would prefer traditional veterinary care, you can consult the directory on the American Veterinary Medical Association (AVMA) website.

Before you decide on a clinic, consider your schedule and where you will go if your dog becomes sick or injured on a holiday or in the middle of the night. Some clinics are only open during the week, while others may be open 7 days a week. The vast majority of clinics are only open during normal business hours, but you may be able to find clinics that are open 24 hours that can handle both routine and emergency care. If you're on a tight budget, research low-cost vaccinations and spaying or neutering in your area.

*Photo Courtesy
of Núria Gort Luna*

What to Expect During the First Visit

Most breeders and shelter staff members recommend taking your new Doberman Pinscher to the vet within the first week or two. The reason for this is to ensure that you have taken home a healthy puppy. A clean bill of health will indicate that the breeder has held up their part of the contract, and any serious illness or injury incurred after this week will not be their responsibility. During your Doberman's first vet visit, you can expect him to undergo a physical examination before he can receive any vaccinations, deworming, or testing. Even if he appears healthy, he will be weighed and have his temperature, heart rate, and respiration measured. The veterinarian will then look him over from teeth to tail to make sure he's as healthy as possible. If your Doberman is still a puppy, he may need vaccine boosters during his first visit, but it will depend on his age and previous veterinary care. The clinic staff will ask you for a record of the Doberman's previous care if you have proof of past vaccinations so that they can enter it into his records. This will also allow them to send out a reminder when your dog is due for his next set of shots.

Puppies typically receive their last round of vaccinations at around 16 weeks of age. Even if your puppy has had one or two vaccinations, it's important to limit his exposure to the outside world until he has been fully vaccinated. Due to their delicate immune system, puppies are at risk of contracting serious illnesses if exposed. It's crucial to avoid public places or introducing your puppy to many human and canine strangers prior to their final shot. Diseases such as parvovirus and distemper can be fatal, so limiting your Doberman's exposure to these illnesses could potentially save his life.

At your Doberman Pinscher's first vet visit, he may also be checked for internal parasites. In order to test for internal parasites, a fecal sample will be collected to examine under a microscope. Under the microscope, any eggs, larvae, worms, or protozoa will be visible. A fecal test is required so that the veterinarian can prescribe the right treatment for the parasites present in your dog's digestive system. Most parasites can be treated with a few doses of medication, usually administered orally or by injection.

The exception to this is heartworm, which is a potentially fatal disease spread by mosquitos. To test for heartworm, which lives in the bloodstream, a small sample of blood must be collected by your veterinarian. If your Doberman tests positive for heartworm, he will need to undergo several months of treatment. During this time, medication is administered at regular intervals, and physical activity must be severely limited. Fortunately, once treatment has been completed, most dogs are able to return to their normal lifestyle with no long-term effects.

You may also want to use your Doberman Pinscher's first vet visit as an opportunity to discuss spaying or neutering. Many vets recommend altering your dog at around six months of age, but some vets prefer to wait until pets are more physically mature. Waiting until dogs are closer to 12-18 months allows most dogs to reach physical maturity before removing their hormones. If your dog has any underlying health conditions, this timeline may also be affected. Your veterinarian will be able to give you an accurate recommendation based on your dog's overall health and lifestyle. If traditional spaying or neutering is not appropriate for your dog, you may also want to ask your veterinarian about alternative procedures such as a vasectomy or ovary-sparing spay. These procedures will allow your Doberman to keep his or her hormones but will prevent any unwanted pregnancies. During this first vet visit, you may also want to ask for a cost estimate for the appropriate procedure so that if you have a tight budget, you can begin to save accordingly.

Caring for Canine Athletes

"Do not exercise any large dog before it is time to feed them OR right after you feed them. The same goes for giving them water before and after exercising. If you do this your dog could get put into Bloat, which can be deadly."

SHARON PFLUEGER
Goldgrove Doberman

Though most of the care given to canine athletes is the same as for pets, there are a few important differences. For most pets, the goal is to keep them healthy and free from disease and injury. However, with dogs bred for sport or work, veterinary care is intended to keep the dog in top condition. A working or sport dog is at a higher risk of developing an injury if his care isn't managed properly. For example, physical examinations for canine athletes go above and beyond the typical exam performed on pets. Veterinarians will also analyze a canine athlete's general fitness level, musculoskeletal structure, and gait. If the vet notices any abnormalities, the dog will need to be closely monitored, or changes will need to be made to his training or physical therapy, depending on the severity of the abnormality.

As an owner of a canine athlete, it's crucial to keep a close eye on your Doberman Pinscher for any sign of lameness, weakness, or change in behavior or performance. These changes can be subtle but must be addressed before they affect the dog's career or performance. The average pet may not

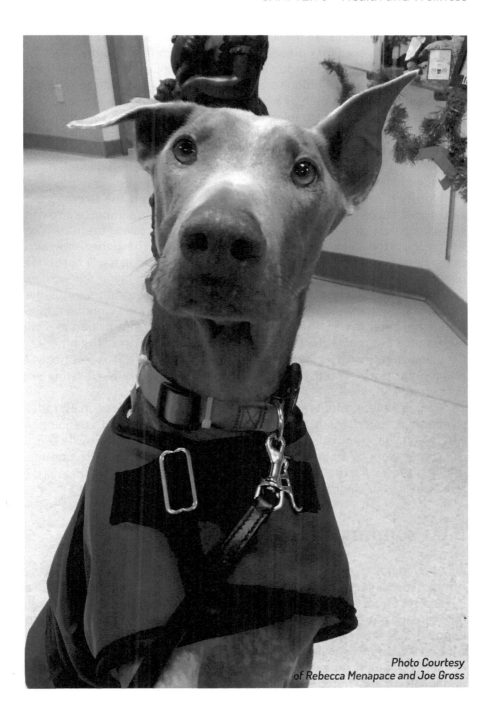

*Photo Courtesy
of Rebecca Menapace and Joe Gross*

need to see a veterinarian for such subtle changes, but working and sport dogs must be treated for potential problems as soon as possible.

If your working or sport dog should become injured, his rehabilitation will need to be carefully monitored to ensure that he is able to return to work. High-drive dogs such as working line Dobermans are prone to reinjury because they have trouble adapting to kennel rest and would prefer to return to their normal activity levels immediately. If your regular veterinarian does not already specialize in treating working dogs, you may want to find one that does or one that specializes in canine rehabilitation and reconditioning.

Nutrition for the canine athlete also differs from the average pet. Nutritional needs may also differ from dog to dog, so it's important to consult a knowledgeable veterinary or canine nutritionist. Even littermates that are placed in the same training program are unlikely to have the same nutritional needs, so it's crucial that your sport or working dog has a nutritional program designed for his specific needs. In order to stay in top working condition, a working or sport dog requires specific nutrients in his diet as well as an increased number of calories based on his workload. Most traditional veterinarians have only a basic education in nutrition and will not be able to provide the care needed for canine athletes. The American College of Veterinary Nutrition (ACVN) has a directory of board-certified veterinary nutritionists on their website if you're having trouble locating one in your area.

Canine athletes often require a team of veterinary professionals, rather than a single veterinarian, in order to stay in peak condition. Depending on where you live, you may have a clinic in your area that can provide everything your working Doberman needs, but you may also have to consider asking professionals at different clinics to work together as a team in order to maintain your canine athlete's health.

Ear Cropping and Tail Docking

Though it is outlawed in much of the rest of the world, tail docking is a common procedure performed on Doberman Pinschers in North America. Regardless of the age of Doberman you bring into your home, he will likely have already had his tail docked, as it is done on puppies just a few days old. Puppies' tails are removed by the breeder or a licensed veterinarian with surgical scissors. The wound is then stitched.

Ear cropping has also been banned in much of the world, but it is still unregulated in the United States and is commonly performed on Dobermans intended for both show and pet homes. The procedure is typically performed between 7 and 9 weeks of age. Most veterinarians advise against cropping after the age of 12 weeks as it's likely that the ears will not stand up.

Both procedures are controversial, though they are signature characteristics of the breed in North America. Though surgical procedures such as spaying and neutering are common, tail docking and ear cropping are often frowned upon because they are purely cosmetic. Docked tails are also at risk of developing a neuroma, or nerve tumor, which can be incredibly painful and cause affected dogs to be very sensitive around their tail. Many opponents of the procedures claim that they interfere with dogs' ability to communicate with other dogs, as tails and ears are used heavily in canine body language.

Whether or not ear cropping and tail docking are appropriate for your new Doberman Pinscher is a decision that must be made between you, your dog's breeder, and your veterinarian. As with any surgery, there are risks associated with anesthesia, and you must decide whether you are willing to accept those risks in exchange for cosmetic appeal.

Dangerous Foods

"Dobermans have a notorious nickname of 'Dobergoat', meaning they will eat many things that are not meant to be ingested. Watch closely to avoid expensive obstruction surgeries!"

DENISE MORMAN
DeMor Dobermans

Most dog owners are aware that certain foods, such as chocolate, caffeine, and alcohol are toxic to their beloved pets. However, there are other lesser-known human foods that can cause serious and potentially fatal health problems as well. Xylitol is a common ingredient in sugar-free candy, gum, and peanut butter and can be lethal if ingested in certain amounts. Onions and garlic contain a substance called N-propyl disulfide that can damage red blood cells. Grapes and raisins are also toxic and can lead to kidney failure, though the exact substance that causes this reaction in dogs has not yet been identified. If your Doberman Pinscher has ingested any of these foods or you suspect that he has eaten something toxic, you need to contact your vet as soon as possible. The more quickly your dog receives treatment, the higher his chances of survival are.

Many types of human foods are not toxic to dogs but should only be fed in moderation, if at all. Peanut butter and cheese are examples of high-fat foods that should only be given sparingly. Not only does excess fat in your

Doberman's diet lead to obesity, but it puts unnecessary stress on his endocrine system and can potentially lead to pancreatitis. Foods that are high in salt, such as bacon, ham, and popcorn, should also be limited or avoided entirely. Lactose-containing foods like ice cream, yogurt, and cottage cheese can also cause digestive upset. Though it may seem obvious, high-sugar foods such as candy and cookies should not be fed as they can cause serious digestive problems.

Common Health Problems in Puppies

Internal parasites are one of the most common health problems found in puppies. It's common for puppies to pick up eggs, larvae, or even adult worms in the womb, through their mother's milk, or through contaminated food, water, soil, or feces. Roundworms, whipworms, tapeworms, and hookworms are among the most common types of internal parasites, though that will vary according to where you live. Heartworms are also common in certain areas, as are protozoa such as giardia and coccidia.

Common symptoms of internal parasites include vomiting, diarrhea, weight loss, and anemia. Puppies with particularly heavy parasite loads will also display a distended stomach and otherwise malnourished-looking body. Coughing and lethargy are also common symptoms of internal parasites but may also be indicative of other illnesses. Some dogs may also display no symptoms at all, so even if your Doberman Pinscher appears to be healthy, you should still have your veterinarian test him periodically for internal parasites.

External parasites like ticks and fleas are also common in puppies. They can be picked up from other pets in the home or any infested outdoor space. Symptoms of fleas and ticks include hair loss, skin inflammation, and severe itching. Dogs affected by fleas may also experience flea allergy dermatitis, which is a reaction by your dog's immune system to the fleas' saliva. Severe anemia and lethargy are also possible with heavy external parasite loads. Fleas can also expose your dog and your family to tapeworms, Lyme disease, bartonellosis, babesiosis, ehrlichiosis, and Rocky Mountain spotted fever. Like many internal parasites, some external parasites are zoonotic and can be passed onto humans, so it's important to treat your dog at the first sign. The area you live in will determine which parasites you may encounter and which diseases they may carry, so talk to your veterinarian about which flea and tick prevention product is right for your Doberman Pinscher.

No matter how carefully you manage your Doberman Pinscher puppy's diet, you will encounter gastrointestinal upset at some point. Puppies are notorious for eating things they shouldn't. Sudden changes in diet and stress

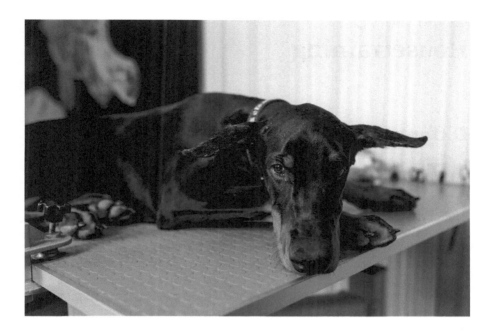

can also cause digestive upset, though some puppies are more sensitive to these changes than others. Vomiting and diarrhea are common symptoms of gastrointestinal upset but rarely have any long-term effect on your dog's health. Most puppies will recover in just a day or two without medical intervention, but if symptoms continue or you see blood in your puppy's stool, it's crucial that you contact your veterinarian as soon as possible. Prolonged digestive upset and bloody stools can be symptoms of serious illness, so you need to seek treatment immediately. If you plan on switching your puppy's food, it's important to do so slowly over a period of about five to ten days. You should also limit the amount of treats, edible chews, and human food you give your puppy, especially if he's undergoing a dietary transition.

CHAPTER 9
Housetraining

Different Options for Housetraining

Now that you've brought your new Doberman Pinscher home, you'll need to decide which of the many housetraining methods and tools that are available you'd like to use. Most owners of large-breed dogs opt for the traditional style of housetraining that teaches your dog to relieve himself outside. Some owners choose to teach their dogs to use certain areas of their yard or garden in order to keep the rest of their outdoor space clean enough for their children or the adults in their home to enjoy. As your Doberman progresses in his housetraining, he'll soon be able to let you know when he needs to go outside by whining, pacing, circling, or pawing at the door. If you like, you can hang housetraining bells on your door, which are a product that has been specifically designed to help dog owners teach their dogs to alert them when they need to go outside.

Photo Courtesy of Amy DeRidder

It's also possible to consider teaching your Doberman Pinscher to use indoor housetraining methods such as puppy pads or potty patches, but these techniques are generally more suitable for small breeds. However, one benefit of these indoor tools is that your dog can take care of his needs while you're away or unavailable to take him outside when he needs to go. Though these options seem impractical with adult Dobermans, they are ideal in helping your puppy transition to relieving himself outdoors while helping to minimize the indoor mess of housetraining.

FUN FACT
Housetraining Large Breeds

A 2019 study lead by Dr. Amy Learn was conducted to determine whether a dog's body size impacts the completeness of housetraining. A survey was posted on surveymonkey.com and received 735 responses from private dog owners. Questions were asked to rule out contributing medical factors and to ascertain whether the dogs were given obedience training. The results showed that large dogs were more likely to be completely house trained than smaller dogs. Further research is needed to understand why this difference might exist.

Disposable or reusable puppy pads or an indoor potty patch are helpful in keeping both your home and puppy cleaner. You can find your option of choice at your local pet store or favorite online retailer. If you're unfamiliar with these products, it's important to familiarize yourself with each to determine which one is best for you and your new dog. Disposable puppy pads are made of plastic and are similar to diapers, though much thinner. They are intended to be tossed in the trash after being soiled and are available in a variety of sizes. However, they can be somewhat wasteful, so many more dog owners are choosing the more environmentally conscious option of reusable puppy pads. They are similar in appearance to disposable pads but are made of several layers of fabric on top of a waterproof base layer. After they are used, they can simply be thrown in the washer just as you would with any other type of laundry. If the pads are quite soiled, or you aren't comfortable washing a dirty pad in your house, you can always hose the pads off outside prior to washing.

Indoor potty patches are another option that can be great for puppies that chew or crumple up puppy pads. They typically consist of a plastic box with a patch of fake grass or turf on top. When your puppy relieves himself on the patch, the urine drains through into the box, which can then be emptied at a later time. Solid waste can be collected from the top and disposed of. Potty patches can become a bit smelly with repeated use, but they are generally quite easy to hose off and sanitize with a pet-friendly disinfectant.

The First Few Weeks

"Dobermans are very smart, but your diligence will be vital during the first several weeks. Every time your puppy wakes up from a nap, he should be immediately taken outside to relieve itself. Every time he urinates or defecates, praise him and tell him what a good boy he is! Give him a good pat and take him back indoors. It is helpful to give him a command word or phrase, such as 'go potty' to begin the training process so he learns what is expected of him."

TRACY DOTY
Halo Dobermans

You're likely to face the most housetraining challenges with your Doberman Pinscher during the first few weeks together. You will not only be facing the challenge of housetraining your new dog, but he'll still be adapting to life in his new home. Remember, patience and consistency are key during this period. When accidents happen, you'll need to remember to stay calm and act appropriately.

Many new dog owners are under the false impression that the best way to correct a dog for having an accident in the home is to rub the dog's nose in it. However, this reaction is unlikely to improve your dog's understanding of your expectations and could even confuse him. Additionally, you risk upsetting your Doberman, especially if he is a young puppy. This is a stressful period for him, and having his face rubbed in his mess by his new family isn't going to help him settle into his new home. If you have discovered that your puppy has made a mess and you were not able to catch him in the act, clean the mess up and move on. Puppies only live in the moment and will not be able to connect the punishment to a crime of the past. If your puppy continuously has accidents in your home and you are not able to catch him, it's likely that his actions are a reflection of your own behavior. Without consistency, your dog will not learn what is expected of him, so if you aren't able to supervise him properly, you need to put him away into his designated area.

If you are able to catch your Doberman in the act of relieving himself indoors, gentle corrections are key. Never hit, yell at, or spank your dog for his mistakes. You'll likely frighten him, and he may instead learn to wait until you aren't watching. Instead, you need to interrupt him with a clap or 'No!' and take him outside right away. Once outside, you can encourage him to finish with calm behavior and a verbal command like 'Go potty!' After he's done, you can reward him with plenty of praise and attention. During this stage of your Doberman's training, over the top affection is a perfectly acceptable response.

The Importance of Consistency

"I always set a timer. Puppy goes out every hour. After eating they go out immediately and if they drink quite a bit of water they go out immediately too. Their bladders are extremely small when they are puppies and they need to go out often. If they have an accident, I blame myself, not the puppy."

DENISE MORMAN
DeMor Dobermans

Photo Courtesy
of Jordan Freeborn

If there is one thing that can singlehandedly determine your Doberman Pinscher's success with housetraining, it's consistency. Consistency is crucial in all aspects of training, but the more consistently you're able to reinforce the rules of the house, the more quickly your dog will learn, and the less frequently he will try to rebel. You need to manage your puppy's environment every moment that he spends outside of his crate or area and never allow him the chance to make a mistake. You will have lapses in your supervision, but the more you're able to monitor and manage your Doberman, the more quickly he'll learn what you expect from him. You need to ensure that your puppy never has unsupervised access to your home. Without supervision, he will be able to relieve himself indoors without consequence, which will only teach him that that is acceptable behavior.

You need to explain this to all human family members to make sure that everyone is on the same page. It can also be helpful for all members of the household to keep track of the puppy's bathroom schedule to help maintain consistency. Some families find that keeping a chart or dry erase board near the puppy's crate or area can be helpful in keeping track of when the puppy went to the bathroom and who was in charge.

As your Doberman Pinscher begins to understand the rules of housetraining and becomes more consistent in relieving himself outdoors, you can begin to relax the rules a bit. However, you shouldn't allow him complete unsupervised freedom in the house until you're certain that he's trustworthy. Whether he's a puppy or an unhousetrained adult, it may be several weeks or several months until you reach this point. Until then, your dog will need to go out every few hours, so be prepared for frequent bathroom breaks. You should always take your dog for a bathroom break after meals, naps, or indoor play sessions.

If you're not quite sure how long your Doberman puppy can hold it between bathroom breaks, you can estimate using his age. For every month of your puppy's age, he should be able to go about an hour between potty breaks. For example, a puppy that is three months old should be able to go about three hours before he needs to go outside. However, no matter what age your new Doberman is, you'll need to start out by taking him out as frequently as every one to two hours when possible. Just because your puppy is physically able to hold it that long, doesn't mean he's willing to do so. This is especially true for unhousetrained adults. Your new Doberman's bathroom schedule should be consistent around the clock until he's old enough to hold it through the night, which usually happens around eight months of age. Until then, be prepared for more than a few sleepless nights.

Positive Reinforcement

As with any aspect of training, positive reinforcement can help your Doberman Pinscher understand your expectations more quickly and readily. As positive reinforcement involves rewarding a dog every time he performs a desired behavior, it's an ideal training method for housetraining. With regular repetition, your dog will begin to happily relieve himself outdoors and may even begin to do so on command.

Again, consistency is crucial with positive reinforcement. At first, your new dog may not connect the tasty treat or loving verbal praise he receives with the action of relieving himself outdoors. Repetition will help him build this association, so it's important for you to set clear expectations for him.

Photo Courtesy of Heather Rosati

The outdoors is an interesting place that begs to be explored, so you'll need to keep your puppy on task for the first few minutes of every trip outside. Use a verbal command, if you'd like, such as 'Go potty.' Stay as calm and serious as possible until your dog has done his job. As he relieves himself, don't interrupt him. Once he's finished, you can praise him with affection, treats, and the opportunity to play or explore. With time, he'll begin to understand that his favorite outdoor activities only happen after he's gone to the bathroom.

Whether you use verbal praise, physical affection, treats, or toys for a reward will depend on your Doberman's individual preferences. Most dogs respond best to food rewards, but many will be happy to perform for attention or playtime. For housetraining, verbal praise and petting generally work best, as it can be difficult to remember to grab the toy or bag of treats on your way out the door every time. However, if your Doberman responds best to a game of tug or a tasty morsel, you'll need to remember his reward each and every time you take him out. Different rewards work best for different dogs, so do whatever your individual dog enjoys most. After his initial reward, you can also allow him time to play or explore on or off leash if your outdoor space allows.

Cleaning Up

"You should expect a few accidents indoors as he is learning, you may offer a 'no' if you catch him in the act and relocate him to the appropriate place to relieve himself, but you should never rub his face or nose in the mess. Patience will be the key in house-training your Doberman. You will start to learn his habits and behaviors and will be able to know to let him out to relieve himself. In the beginning, make it your habit of taking him outside as soon as he gets up in the morning, after he eats, after naps and before bedtime."

TRACY DOTY
Halo Dobermans

Even if your Doberman Pinscher's housetraining is going as smoothly as possible, you're guaranteed to have at least a few messes to clean up. To help minimize reoccurrences and prevent stains and odors, you need to use the right type of cleaning product. First, it's important to consider what types of floors you have in your home. Urine can leave lasting stains and odors, and feces can contain dangerous bacteria and even parasites, so it's crucial to use the right product for your flooring to ensure that they are properly cleaned and sanitized. Most cleaners are labeled for the types of flooring they should be used on. Many pet mess cleaners contain special enzymes to help break down odor-causing particles that might tempt your new dog to return to the same spot.

Once you've purchased your cleaning product of choice, you'll also need to stock up on cleaning rags, paper towels, and scrub brushes. Paper towels are an easy way to clean up messes and dispose of them, but they're not ideal for scrubbing as they will fall apart. Depending on the number of messes you're cleaning up, it can also feel a bit wasteful to toss so many paper towels in the trash. Fabric towels or rags are more durable and can be used for

Photo Courtesy
of Susie Garcia

scrubbing. They can also be washed after use rather than disposed of. For hard surfaces like tile or linoleum, a scrub brush can make cleaning easier, especially if you need to clean grout between tiles. Depending on the type of flooring you have, you might also consider using a household steam cleaner to clean and sanitize. However, it's important to make sure your flooring is properly sealed as steam can cause water damage to unsealed floors.

If you have carpeted floors in your home, you're obviously in for more of a challenge. Before cleaning up any messes, consider testing your cleaning product of choice in an inconspicuous area to check for discoloration. Avoid using scrub brushes and instead opt for fabric towels or rags. Also, avoid vigorous scrubbing as you may accidentally cause your carpet to unravel. If you can't seem to get rid of stains or odors on your carpets, consider discussing your problem areas with a professional carpet cleaning service.

Playpens and Doggy Doors

As your Doberman Pinscher progresses in his housetraining, you can begin trusting him with more space and responsibility over his bathroom schedule. Using a playpen when you're unable to fully supervise him is an excellent intermediate step that can give him more freedom and space, while still limiting his access to your entire home. You may not want to leave him in the playpen when you leave the house, but it can easily be used to keep him contained while you're busy with work, household chores, or family activities. If you want your Doberman to have more space to stretch his legs, but he isn't yet housetrained, consider lining his playpen with reusable or disposable puppy pads to help minimize messes. When shopping for playpens, you'll need to choose one that is tall enough that your Doberman can't climb or jump over the panels and is sturdy enough not to be knocked down.

If your outdoor space allows and you're ready to give your Doberman Pinscher more control over his bathroom needs, a doggy door can be a great housetraining tool. Doggy doors allow your puppy or adult dog to take himself outside any time he chooses, rather than relying on you to take him out. Your local pet store or favorite online retailer likely has several styles to choose from, so you'll need to decide if a temporary or permanent installation suits your needs. Temporary doggy doors can be installed in most sliding glass doors and can be easily removed when needed with no lasting effects on the door or frame.

Permanent doggy doors can be installed in both wooden and metal doors, or they can be placed in any wall. Both temporary and permanent doors can be locked, so you can limit your dog's access and keep your home secure while you're away. Many types also rely on a small tag worn by your dog that unlocks the door when he approaches. Once your dog goes through the door, it returns to the locked position to prevent your other pets, neighborhood strays, or wild animals from going through.

When shopping for doggy doors, choose an appropriate size for your Doberman Pinscher; this can be difficult if he's still a puppy. You can always use a temporary door until he reaches his adult size, when a more permanent solution can be installed. It's also possible to choose a door appropriate for your dog's approximate adult size, but it's important to be aware that larger doors have heavier flaps that may be difficult for small puppies to go through. If you choose a door smaller than your dog's adult size, he may be forced to squeeze through an uncomfortably tight space, so make sure you choose the right size.

It's also important that you make sure your outdoor space is completely secure prior to allowing your Doberman unsupervised access with his new doggy door. Even if you puppy-proofed the yard when you first brought your dog home, it's worth going through once more to check for open gates, holes in the fence, or any other potential danger. Remember, adult Dobermans are more than capable of climbing over fences as tall as six feet, so if you're worried about your dog becoming a flight risk, you might reconsider investing in a doggy door.

CHAPTER 10
Socialization

The Importance of Good Socialization

"To begin, socialize with only one dog at a time. Too many dogs together can be intimidating especially for a young dog. Make sure above all else the other dog you are socializing with is friendly towards other dogs!"

ELAINE HOPPER
Starlaine Dobermans

Though there are many benefits to properly socializing your Doberman Pinscher. One of the most obvious is that you'll be able to take him with you almost anywhere and trust him to behave. Not only will you have more confidence in his ability to handle himself, but he'll have more confidence as well. This is especially important if you plan on showing or competing

with your Doberman, but even if your goals are as simple as taking your dog along to meet a friend for coffee at the local café, socialization is crucial. It's worth noting that socialization is not a one-time event that will prepare your dog for a lifetime of friendly encounters. Dobermans can be naturally wary of strangers, so socialization will need to continue throughout your new companion's life.

Good socialization is also essential to your dog's overall wellbeing. Dobermans are incredibly loyal dogs that love spending time with their people, so the more that you can

HISTORY
Sauer the Tracker

Sauer, a Doberman Pinscher, was born in 1917 in South Africa near Cape Town, on the grounds of the South African Police Dog School. Sauer came from an impressive lineage but struggled with police work. Sauer's trainer, Detective-Sergeant Herbert Kruger, eventually was successful in harnessing Sauer's tracking abilities. The dog once followed a trail that was 132 hours old, and in 1925 tracked a cattle rustler for 100 miles on foot through the Great Karoo desert, and was successful in apprehending the thief. Sauer passed away at the age of nine and holds the world record for tracking.

include your dog in your family's day to day activities, the better. It's also a great source of mental stimulation and, in many cases, physical exercise as well. Meeting new people and canine playmates is sure to improve your dog's physical health and happiness. Remember, physical and mental stimulation is key in preventing destructive bad habits caused by boredom, so the benefits of socialization go far beyond the obvious.

Without proper socialization, your Doberman is at risk of becoming fearful, aggressive, or simply unpredictable. It can be hard to predict how an overstimulated dog is going to react in any given situation, and your dog could become a liability if he reacts aggressively. Poorly socialized adult dogs can also be incredibly difficult for the average owner to manage on their own. If you've brought home a puppy, you should be aware that socialization can become more challenging as your Doberman ages, so be sure to start as soon as your puppy is fully vaccinated and medically cleared by your veterinarian.

Socialization is essential to all dogs, so whether you've purchased your Doberman for sport or have rescued a family companion, proper socialization will make your lives much easier. A well-socialized dog will be easy to walk around the neighborhood as you won't need to worry about him barking and lunging at everyone you encounter. Every dog will also need to visit veterinarians, groomers, or boarding facilities at some point in their lives, and the better socialized your dog is, the easier he will be for professionals to handle and care for.

Socializing Puppies

"You should plan to take your puppy on short walks in public places where he will see other people and other dogs, as well as hear unfamiliar sounds. You should take special precaution with other dogs, they aren't always friendly. It is a great idea to attend puppy kindergarten classes, which will not only help with socialization, but will also help teach him good manners and can serve as a basis for future training."

TRACY DOTY
Halo Dobermans

Many reputable breeders believe in starting socialization as early as possible through methods like Puppy Culture, which prepares puppies for their lives with their future new owners. However, you'll need to continue the socialization process after bringing your new Doberman Pinscher home. This can be difficult with particularly young puppies, which are often

Photo Courtesy
of Eileen Pryor

unvaccinated or undervaccinated. Until your Doberman puppy has received all of his vaccinations, including rabies, you'll need to limit his exposure to the outside world while still moving forward with socialization. Even within your home, you can expose him to new sights, sounds, and experiences. Taking advantage of your outdoor spaces, you can even introduce him to different surfaces such as bare soil, grass, concrete, and wooden planks. Don't be afraid to get creative around your home until it's safe to take your new Doberman out in public.

Part of your new puppy's socialization should include handling to get him used to the experiences of being at the vet or groomer. The more that you're able to do at home with your puppy, the less stressful these experiences will be later in life. Even though you can't take your puppy out on the town during the first few months, you can still lay the foundation for lifelong socialization. Once your puppy has a basic understanding of how to deal with new experiences, and once he has been fully vaccinated, you can begin to build on that foundation outside of the home.

After your puppy has been cleared by your vet for outside experiences, you need to introduce him to as many new people, places, and animals as you can. Begin taking your Doberman for brief car rides just to get him used to it. Running errands or visiting a friend for a puppy playdate can be a great way to include him in your daily activities and introduce him to new experiences. You might also consider signing up for a puppy obedience class. You can also begin inviting guests over so your puppy can get used to the idea of having strangers in his home without reacting out of stress, overexcitement, or fear.

Although it's important to expose your Doberman Pinscher to as many new things as possible, it's crucial that you also look out for his mental well-being. You don't want to accidentally frighten or overwhelm him. To set your dog up for socialization success, you need to ensure that he only has positive experiences. It only takes a single negative experience to undo months of socialization, so use caution and go as slow as you need to. If you notice fearful or uncomfortable body language in your puppy, back off and go more slowly. There will be a time to encourage your puppy to work through his fear, but for now, you need to make sure his experiences are all positive.

It's not uncommon for new dog owners to take their puppies to the local dog park to socialize them, but the uncontrolled chaos can leave a lasting negative impression on many puppies. Instead, try to plan playdates for your puppy with just one or two new dogs at a time. Make sure the dogs in question are friendly and gentle toward puppies. Your Doberman's success in socialization is your responsibility, so you need to manage his environment appropriately.

Socializing Adult Dogs

In many ways, adopting an adult Doberman Pinscher can be easier than raising a puppy, but it's important to be aware of how challenging it can be to socialize adult dogs compared to puppies. With puppies, you need only to make sure they have consistently positive experiences. However, with adults, you may need to overcome past trauma, some that you may not even be aware of. Though there may be cases where an adult dog's entire history is known, most of the time it remains somewhat of a mystery. This means that your new Doberman's behavior may appear to be unpredictable at times, so it's best to start slow and not make any assumptions about his previous experiences. Even if the shelter or breeder informs you that the dog is well-socialized, it's still important to be cautious so that you aren't caught off guard by anything.

Just as with puppies, it's crucial to make sure that your adult Doberman Pinscher is only put into situations that will leave a positive impression on him. That means you should introduce him to just one or two friendly new dogs at a time. If you aren't sure of how friendly a new dog is, it's best to avoid introduction until you're more confident of your new dog's ability to handle himself in social situations. If you accidentally place your dog into a situation where he feels frightened or overwhelmed, you may lose his trust in you as a leader, so proceed with caution. In many cases, your best bet may

Photo Courtesy
of Shannon Westmoreland

be to let your Doberman observe new situations from afar and approach only if he displays calm and relaxed body language. More information on how to properly introduce dogs will be provided in the next chapter.

If your adult Doberman Pinscher has had negative experiences in his past, you'll need to be patient and understanding as you work on socialization. Though it can be easy to become frustrated at your new dog's lack of progress, focus on staying patient and consistent in his training. If at any time you feel underqualified for his reactivity or behavioral problems, don't be afraid to contact a professional trainer or behaviorist. It's best to seek help as soon as possible rather than allow the behavior to potentially escalate.

Lifelong Socialization

"Socialization is very important; I encourage all of my puppy people to bring their puppy with them everywhere, from Home Depot to Tractor Supply to your child's soccer game, the more places you go the more socialized your puppy will be."

SHARON DUVAL
Kettle Cove Dobermans

As mentioned previously, socialization is something that will need to continue throughout your Doberman Pinscher's life. Even if you socialize your puppy well, all your efforts may be in vain if you drop the ball as he reaches adulthood. Part of good socialization is eventually exposing your dog to situations where he may feel frightened or nervous. These experiences are an essential part of strengthening your bond and allowing him to trust that you'll keep him safe. Not only will this help with future socialization, but other aspects of training as well. If you stop socializing your Doberman at any point in his life or allow him into too many situations where he feels uncomfortable, you can lose his trust. Socialization must be done correctly and consistently throughout your dog's lifetime.

Lifelong socialization is also a key aspect of providing your dog with adequate mental and physical exercise. The more frequently you expose him to new situations, the more he gets to use his brain to decide how to handle the varying challenges. Including your dog in your daily activities is also a great way of giving him more physical exercise. Not only will your Doberman enjoy spending as much time with you as possible, but the stimulation and socialization it provides will help to prevent him from developing boredom-related bad habits.

Same-Sex Aggression

If you currently have multiple dogs or plan to have multiple dogs in the future, it's important to be aware of the high rate of same-sex aggression in the Doberman Pinscher breed. Though your new Doberman might get along well with dogs of any gender, it's important to still be aware of the risks associated with same-sex aggression.

In a study done by the American Veterinary Medical Association (AVMA) on a selection of various dog breeds, it was discovered that about 79% of aggression between dogs of the same household involved same-sex pairs. Of those same-sex pairs, approximately 68% were female. However, many Doberman owners have anecdotally noted that much of the same-sex aggression in the breed is found between male pairs. It was also estimated that around 70% of the incidents were instigated by the younger or newer dog and that the majority of fights were triggered by resource guarding behavior. Other triggers found to cause fights between same-sex pairs included excitement or overstimulation and the owner paying more attention to one dog.

It should be noted that same-sex aggression is generally unrelated to whether or not a dog has been spayed or neutered. It's possible for an individual dog to show same-sex aggression regardless of whether or not it has been altered. Additionally, spaying or neutering is unlikely to reduce or eliminate same-sex aggression, so if an unaltered dog displays aggression to a dog of the same gender, it's unlikely that the behavior will disappear if the dog undergoes surgical alteration.

Most reputable breeders and rescues familiar with the breed are unlikely to place a Doberman in a home with another dog of the same sex. It's possible that you may be denied adoption of a dog of the same sex in the future after you've adopted your Doberman Pinscher due to the prevalence of this behavior in the breed.

Same-sex aggression is a serious behavioral problem that can result in serious injuries and even the death of one or both dogs. Additionally, human members of the family are put at risk should they decide to intervene or attempt to break up the fight. Doberman Pinschers are large and powerful dogs, and their fights can be vicious.

In a variety of studies performed on same-sex aggression, researchers discovered that proper training, management, and behavior modification could make a difference in 57% to 75% of same-sex pairs. In nearly all cases, owners dealing with same-sex aggression worked with professional trainers or behaviorists to reduce conflict and improve behavior. If you're dealing with same-sex aggression in your home, it's crucial to seek help as soon as possible. Neglecting the situation can lead to tragic consequences. It's also important to be aware that not all same-sex aggression cases can be solved. In some situations, it may be better to rehome one or both dogs so that their behavioral needs can be adequately met.

Dealing with High Prey Drives

It's not uncommon for Doberman Pinschers, especially individuals from working bloodlines, to have high prey drives. While this can be helpful in training, it can make socialization with small animals quite difficult. The natural instincts of a dog with a high prey drive are often triggered by the fast movement of prey animals, so you should use caution any time your Doberman is around small animals while off leash. You should also be careful about allowing your new dog to be off leash in any unfenced area as it's possible that he may be so focused on pursuing a squirrel or rabbit he may not hear your recall command. This could put him in danger of running into the road or through other potentially dangerous areas.

Your Doberman's prey drive is not likely to be restricted to wild animals such as squirrels. Small dogs and cats can also trigger a dog's prey drive, so even if your dog seems friendly toward such animals at first, he may become aggressive if they try to run from him. Socialization with small animals is best started at a young age, so if you've brought home a puppy, now is the time to get him used to being around small animals. If you've adopted an adult Doberman, you'll need to be more cautious as he may have already developed that chasing behavior. It's also possible that your Doberman may not ever be able to be around small animals while off leash. Some dogs have too strong of a prey drive to see any small animal as anything other than prey. If this is true for your dog, it's important to manage his environment carefully to make sure he's never in a situation where he could accidentally hurt another animal.

Controlling your Doberman Pinscher's prey drive should be an essential part of his training. In order for him to behave reliably off leash, you want to discourage him from chasing small animals and focus on you instead. Never yell at your Doberman or jerk his leash to draw his attention away. If he's focused on potential prey, he will probably ignore you anyway. Instead, offer him a high-value treat to encourage him to focus on you rather than trying to punish him for focusing elsewhere. It can be helpful to use a command such as 'Look!' to gain his focus, but this is best practiced first in situations without any distractions. After you have your dog's attention, you can ask him to perform other tasks to keep him distracted. With practice and consistency, you should be able to gain your dog's attention no matter how distracting his surroundings are.

Dealing with Fear

"I tell my puppy buyers DO NOT go to dog parks as you do not know the health of the other dogs, or their temperament. The negative side of that is you could ruin the temperament of your pup if you run into a nasty dog owned by someone else!"

SHARON PFLUEGER
Goldgrove Doberman

No matter how carefully you manage your Doberman Pinscher's socialization, it's almost guaranteed that you're going to eventually encounter a situation that triggers your dog's fear. These are important learning opportunities that must be handled carefully to avoid traumatizing your dog. Instead of leaving a lasting negative impression on your dog, you can use these situations to gain your dog's trust and give him confidence.

In order to handle your Doberman's fear appropriately, it's important to be aware of his body language at all times. Signs of nervousness or fear include tucking the tail under the body, panting, trembling, licking the lips, yawning, flattening the ears, and avoidance. These are relatively mild signs, and most dogs that display this type of body language can be

Photo Courtesy of Brooklyn Burnz

kept under control and calmed down or distracted. However, if left unaddressed, fear can escalate to pacing and attempting to escape. These are signs of serious anxiety and must be addressed before your dog panics. It's common for panicked dogs to lash out aggressively if they feel they need to protect themselves, so you need to take earlier signs seriously.

One of the most important aspects of working through your Doberman's fear is keeping your own behavior under control. If you act nervous or begin to panic, your dog will react knowing there is a reason to be afraid. However, if you stay calm and collected, he's more likely to calm down and trust you to protect him. Even if you don't necessarily feel that way, it's important to act with confidence. You should also avoid trying to comfort your dog in times of fear. It can be tempting to coddle him when he becomes nervous, but all you're doing is reassuring him that there is a reason for him to be afraid. Attempting to correct your dog's behavior won't help either. Instead, you need to show your Doberman that you're not afraid and behave calmly and confidently to set an example. By minimizing your reactions, you're letting your dog know that he has nothing to fear, and you have everything handled.

After a fearful situation is over, it's important to reflect on the situation. If the result was positive, and you were able to calm your dog and work through his fear, you may not need to handle future situations differently. However, if you were unable to calm your dog, you may need to reflect on what went wrong. This is a learning opportunity for you both, so it's important to learn from your mistakes in order to develop your training skills.

It's also important to recognize when things have escalated beyond your control. If you believe that you are unable or unwilling to handle your Doberman's fear on your own, consult a professional as soon as possible. Fear is a behavior that can escalate quickly if left unaddressed, so contact a trainer or behaviorist immediately. It can take months or years to overcome serious fear issues, so the sooner you seek help, the sooner you can begin working on a solution. Remember, patience, consistency, and the willingness to seek professional help when needed are key in overcoming difficult behavioral problems.

CHAPTER 11
The Multi-pet Household

Introducing a Puppy to Other Animals

When you already have one or more pets in your home, introducing a new dog can be stressful. Although every owner prays that introductions go as smoothly as possible, it's not always the case, so you need to be prepared with a plan of action. If you're introducing a puppy into the home, it's typically the adult already living in the household that you'll need to worry about. Even if they are a bit nervous at first, most puppies are happy to get along with everyone, whereas adult dogs will vary in their reactions toward puppies.

When introducing your Doberman Pinscher to animals in your household, no matter what species the other animals may be, proper restraint is crucial to the safety of everyone involved. For your Doberman, a collar and leash may be fine, but in some cases, a harness may be the better choice as you will be able to grab your puppy and remove him from the situation without the risk of

Photo Courtesy of Jamie Adkins

injuring him by pulling suddenly on his collar. For livestock or smaller animals such as poultry, a sturdy fence should work well. Even if there is a fence, it's still a good idea to keep your Doberman on a leash, just to prevent him from trying to climb over or through the fence or chase the animals along the fence line. This way, your puppy and the other animals can see and smell each other, but with a barrier to prevent potential injuries if one or both become frightened or overwhelmed.

FUN FACT
Therapy Dogs

When you think of working Dobermans, the first thought that comes to mind is usually that of a guard dog. But Dobermans are increasingly being used as therapy and service dogs. Their intelligence and loyalty make Dobermans an excellent choice for therapy work, including hospital therapy, PTSD therapy, and seizure alert work. They are also often used as search and rescue dogs, as well as guide dogs for the blind.

Regardless of how friendly your existing animals are, it's important to go slowly with introductions. Start by allowing the animals to watch each other from a distance and bring them closer as they feel more comfortable. For indoor introductions, a seldom-used room may be the most quiet and convenient place to introduce your pets. For outdoor introductions, it's important that no animal is cornered and has room to step away if they get nervous. You need to monitor both your dog's body language and that of the animal you're introducing him to for signs of fear, anxiety, or aggression. If you see anything that could escalate, separate the animals immediately. For some animals, it can take several introductory sessions for them to become acquainted, so don't be too concerned if they don't appear to like each other at first.

In the first few weeks or even months, never allow your Doberman Pinscher puppy to be left alone with your other animals without proper supervision. Accidents can happen quickly and with little warning, so you need to be present and watching their body language until you are absolutely certain that they can be trusted together.

As discussed in Chapter 10, some Dobermans have higher prey drives than others, so you need to use extra caution when introducing your puppy to small animals like rodents, cats, poultry, or even small dogs. The likelihood of your puppy becoming comfortable around these animals without trying to chase or hurt them is higher if you can begin introductions at a young age, but there are dogs that will never be able to be trusted around prey animals. Until you get to know your new Doberman better and can predict how he will react around small animals, it's best to err on the side of caution. Training can improve a dog's impulse control, but you still may not be able to trust your Doberman to behave himself in your absence.

Introducing an Adult Dog to Other Animals

While there are many similarities between introducing a puppy and an adult dog to other animals, there are also some key differences. As previously mentioned, the main difference is that the history of adult dogs is often unknown, so it can be difficult to predict how they will behave. When introducing your adult Doberman Pinscher to your other animals, you'll need to use a bit more caution than you would with a puppy.

As with puppies, restraint is an essential aspect of safe introductions, no matter what species you're dealing with. An adult Doberman can be capable of seriously injuring another animal should he escape your restraint, so you need to make sure he is secure. A glancing kick from a large animal such as a horse can seriously injure your Doberman as well, so you need to prioritize everyone's safety. Adult Dobermans are large and powerful enough to knock or pull over a child or small adult, so you also need to make sure that you are strong enough to keep your dog under control if necessary.

Again, you'll need to proceed slowly with introductions and make sure each animal is comfortable before closing the distance between the two. If you go slowly, you'll be able to separate the animals or back off before their behavior escalates, and they become more difficult to control. If your Doberman appears to react with fear or aggression consistently, or you're having trouble keeping him under control, you need to seek professional help. A professional trainer or behaviorist that specializes in reactive dogs will be able to help you correct your dog's behavior and ensure the safety of all animals and humans in your home.

Photo Courtesy of Rebecca Menapace and Joe Gross

Photo Courtesy
of Christopher and Amber Sterner

Fighting and Bad Behavior

If your Doberman Pinscher ever displays aggressive behavior, you need to act immediately, as aggression can escalate quickly if not corrected. A dog will never start a fight with another dog unless his warning signs have been ignored. It can be easy to ignore that growl when one dog comes too close to another dog's favorite sleeping spot or that play sessions starts to get too rough. However, without immediate intervention, that small sign of aggression is certain to escalate each and every time it occurs, and a fight will eventually break out. Dog fights can cause serious injuries, especially if there is a significant size difference between the dogs involved. Resource guarding and bullying should not be tolerated, no matter which animal is the cause. Dogs should be allowed to have some personal boundaries, but they should be reasonable. If your dog begins to display aggressive behavior, you need to interrupt with a loud 'No!', clap, or stomp. This distraction may be enough to draw your dog's attention away from the situation.

Photo Courtesy
of Angela Munden

Aggressive body language will be obvious once you know what to look for. An overtly aggressive dog will stand tall, with his head high above his shoulders. His body will be tense, and he may be leaning forward toward the other dog. He may show his teeth, and his eyes will be locked on his opponent. Some dogs will also raise their hackles, which is the hair along the top of his neck and back. At this stage, a fight is likely imminent without intervention. However, aggression in its early stages may be as subtle as a stiffened posture and intense eye contact. At this stage, the behavior can typically be corrected without further aggression. It's important to understand what the various stages of aggression look like so you can intervene to prevent a fight.

It's also crucial to determine the underlying cause of the aggression because without this information, you'll never be able to fully correct your dog's aggressive behavior. Every time your Doberman shows aggressive body language, take note of his environment and what the other dog is doing that could be causing your dog to react this way. If your dog becomes aggressive over sharing food or toys, you may need to feed him separately or remove toys from the house. Resource guarding can be difficult to correct without professional help but knowing that is what's causing the problem will help you to determine the correct path forward. Other potential causes of fights include sharing attention, rough play, and dominant behavior.

If your Doberman's aggressive behavior ever does escalate, use extreme caution when breaking up a fight. No matter how gentle they are most of the time, most dogs are so focused on the fight that they may lash out at you. Some fights can be broken up with little effort, while others may require more extreme measures. For minor fights, loud noises may be enough of a distraction to break up the fight. This is one of the few situations where it's permissible to yell at your dogs. You can also try stomping, clapping, or even banging metal dog dishes together. Throwing a bowl of water at the dogs or spraying them with a hose may also work.

If you absolutely must physically break up the fight, you need to decide which dog is the aggressor and which is defending himself. If you are alone, grab the aggressor by the back legs and pull him away from the other dog. You have the option of either pulling straight back or swinging him to the side, but you need to move him quickly to prevent him from turning around and biting you. If you have someone with you who is able to help, they can perform the same maneuver on the other dog. Once the dogs have been pulled apart, quickly restrain and separate them to prevent them from rejoining the fight.

In some fights, dogs may bite down on one another and refuse to let go. Never try to pull their jaws apart with your bare hands. If spraying the dogs with water won't get them to let go, you can try prying their jaws apart with a wedge-shaped item such as a doorstop. You can even buy a product called a break stick, which is a wedge-shaped piece of wood designed to pry open a dog's mouth. Break sticks can be purchased at any store specializing in training equipment. If you're using a break stick, make sure your hands are far enough away from the dog's mouth that he can't bite you if he tries to regrip.

Aggression and fighting are serious behavioral issues that can be difficult, if not impossible, for the average dog owner to manage alone. Fights are not only dangerous to the dogs involved but may put your human family members at risk if they try to intervene. As the owner of an aggressive dog, it's crucial to be able and willing to recognize when you are no longer able to control the situation and seek professional help immediately. Aggression will not get better without immediate professional guidance, and if you cannot correct the behavior on your own, you need to contact a trainer or behaviorist before a tragedy occurs.

Raising Multiple Puppies from the Same Litter

Bringing home two or more Doberman Pinschers from the same litter may seem like a great idea, especially if you don't have any other pets at home. After all, littermates have been together since birth, so you won't need to worry about introductions, and your dogs will never be left home alone since they'll have their sibling for companionship. Plus, your dogs will never be bored since they will always have a playmate ready to keep them busy while you do household chores or are away at work or school.

However, it's important to consider all of the challenges associated with raising multiple puppies. More puppies mean more trouble, more training, and more of a time commitment. Littermates having a great bond already can be helpful when bringing them home for the first time, but if you need to separate them, for separate vet visits, for example, they may react with anxiety and panic. Dogs that have never been on their own can be incredibly reactive and fearful, and the one left at home may resort to destructive behaviors to cope with his anxiety. Housetraining will also be more difficult, and breaking bad habits will be incredibly challenging. You'll also have double the food and vet bills.

If you work full-time, have family commitments, and enjoy having a personal life, you may want to reconsider bringing home multiple puppies. Puppies around the same age, regardless of whether they're actually littermates, may develop Littermate Syndrome. Littermate Syndrome is a collection of behaviors displayed by puppies raised in the same household. It's not uncommon for one puppy to become increasingly withdrawn or introverted. The puppies usually end up being incredibly co-dependent and generally do not bond to their humans as strongly as a single puppy would. It's also common for puppies with Littermate Syndrome to begin fighting as they mature. For this reason, most trainers and breeders recommend against

Photo Courtesy
of Michelle Rickard

HELPFUL TIP
A Well-Trained Doberman

The key to having a gentle and friendly Doberman who is more likely to get along with other dogs, both in and out of the home, is good training and socialization. Different dogs will have different personalities, and some dogs may be more naturally inclined to get along with other pets, but proper training goes a long way toward preparing your dog for sharing space with other dogs and pets.

bringing home one or more puppies from the same litter. In fact, most reputable breeders will not allow two or more puppies from a litter to go to the same home.

If you're concerned about your Doberman Pinscher being alone at home but aren't equipped to deal with the potential challenges associated with raising littermates, consider adopting one puppy first. Once he reaches an age where you feel he has been trained and socialized enough to set a good example, you can consider bringing home a second puppy. This way, your dog will only be alone for several months or a year of his life, but he will be bonded to you and have enough training that you will be free to shift your focus to a new puppy when the time comes.

Options if Your Pets Don't Get Along

No matter how hard you try to make sure your pets get along, it's entirely possible that they may never be able to coexist. Some animals may not be interested in friends, especially if they've been an only pet for most of their lives. Older pets can be especially resistant to getting along with new dogs. Before you make any serious decisions, make sure that you aren't rushing introductions and have given the animals enough time to familiarize themselves. Patience and a commitment to training are essential in helping animals to live comfortably together. You may also want to seek the advice of a professional trainer or behaviorist.

However, if you're out of options and your pets refuse to get along, you may need to make a decision. It can be heartbreaking to give up a pet but keeping two pets that refuse to coexist is a serious commitment that should not be taken lightly. You will need to keep them separate to ensure each pet's safety, while also ensuring they both receive adequate exercise, care, and affection. Each dog will require a comfortable space to retreat to where he cannot come into contact with the other. This type of lifestyle can be stressful for both pets and humans in the household. It can be exhaust-ing and time-consuming as well, so it's crucial that you seriously consider whether you're able or willing to provide this type of care for as long as your pets may live.

Don't be ashamed if you admit that you are unable or unwilling to endure this type of lifestyle. It's perfectly acceptable to admit that you can't do it, no matter how much you love your pets. If this is the case, you may need to find one of them a new home. There is nothing to be ashamed about if this is the best option for your pets and your family. Some pets simply prefer single-pet environments, while others just need a different type of lifestyle in order for them to thrive. Though this decision can be utterly heartbreaking, it is your responsibility to make the right choice regarding what is best for your animals.

CHAPTER 12
Training Your Doberman Pinscher

"The Doberman is a highly intelligent breed. They will learn quickly and benefit from positive reinforcement. They will learn to resent an owner that is overly negative when training and will fail to reach their potential. With this intelligence comes the ability to bore easily. You should keep your training sessions short but frequent. It is a great idea to find a local training class in your area and sign up! You will be amazed to see how quickly your dog will respond to positive training. A well trained, well mannered dog will be a joy to live with and a wonderful companion."

TRACY DOTY
Halo Dobermans

Photo Courtesy of Aly Sandahl

Benefits of Proper Training

"The correct Doberman Pinscher 'owns the ground it stands on' so a new owner needs to be consistent and reinforce good behavior with lots of praise. Negative attention from the new owner to the dog will result in escalating poor behaviors from the dog."

PAMELA DEHETRE
Pamelot, Reg.

Not only will frequent and proper training sessions help your Doberman Pinscher to become a well-behaved member of the family, but it's also a great way to keep him busy and prevent bad behavior caused by boredom. Frequent sessions as short as five or ten minutes several times per day are enough to provide the mental stimulation your dog needs each day. Most healthy, fit dogs can walk or play for hours and still be energetic enough to tire you out, but it's more exhausting for your dog to have to work his mind. This is why even short training sessions can wear your dog out quickly.

Remember, a dog who regularly exercises both his mind and body will be calmer and better behaved in the house.

What you teach your Doberman Pinscher in each training session will depend on what you plan to do with him. If you adopted a Doberman as an active family companion, basic obedience would help him adjust to life with his new family. If you've purchased a Doberman with the intent of competing in dog sports, you may want to start with basic obedience and move on to more sport-related commands. Additionally, tricks are a fun way to keep your dog's mind busy while also entertaining your friends and family. Whatever you choose to teach your dog, the benefits of regular training sessions will help you build the bond you've always dream of.

Operant Conditioning Basics

"Most importantly you should always remember to include praise as a part of training. A happy dog that feels like it is succeeding will progress through training much easier and much more quickly. A Doberman is devoted to his owner and seeks his owner's approval."

TRACY DOTY
Halo Dobermans

One of the most frequently used methods of learning utilized by professional dog trainers is operant conditioning. Known as the father of operant conditioning, American psychologist and behaviorist B.F. Skinner originally developed his theory of operant conditioning based on the idea that humans and animals are complex creatures that must be able to learn through more than classical conditioning alone. He believed that if specific behaviors were followed by positive experiences, the animal or human would be more likely to repeat the behavior in the future. On the other hand, if the behaviors were followed by negative experiences, the learner would be less likely to repeat the behavior again.

Skinner also believed that there are three environmental responses that shape behavior: neutral operants, reinforcers, and punishments. Neutral operants are environmental responses that have no influence on whether a learner will repeat the behavior in the future. An example of a neutral operant is if you respond to your dog's behavior by taking a sip of coffee. Your response is unlikely to have any effect on your dog's behavior and is thus considered a neutral operant. Reinforcers increase the likelihood of learners repeating specific behaviors and can be either positive or negative. Positive reinforcers

FUN FACT
Bond, Doberman Bond

The 1979 James Bond film, "Moonraker", features two dogs who may have been Dobermans. The intimidating pooches belong to the movie's villain, Huge Drax, who sicks them after his secretary after he fires her. There is some controversy surrounding the breed of these dogs and whether or not they are Dobermans. Some believe that the dogs featured in the film are actually Beaucerons, a breed that is often mistaken for the Doberman.

include food, playtime, praise, and petting. Negative reinforcers are defined by the removal of an unpleasant sensation, such as gentle pressure on the leash. Punishments reduce the likelihood of the learner repeating the specific behavior in the future and can range from mildly unpleasant to painful. Examples of punishments in dog training include the word 'No' and loud noises such as claps and stomps. Painful punishments should never be used with any dog as they can permanently damage a dog's mind and body.

Positive Reinforcement

Most people are familiar with the concept of positive reinforcement in terms of dog training. It's one of the most common methods of teaching dogs as they are highly motivated by food and praise. Positive reinforcement is used to encourage dogs to repeat desired behaviors by rewarding them with a treat, marker, or verbal praise. Unfortunately, desired behaviors are not the only thing dogs can learn through positive reinforcement. Bad habits that are self-rewarding, such as raiding the trash can, can be picked up quickly once a dog realizes there are tasty treats inside the trash. As your dog's caretaker, you must manage his environment appropriately to prevent him from having the opportunity to experience the rewards of naughty behavior.

Negative Reinforcement

It's important to note that there is a difference between punishments and negative reinforcement. When used in combination with positive reinforcement, negative reinforcement can be a great way to help your dog understand what's being asked of him. Remember, negative reinforcers are the removal of unpleasant sensations. When used correctly, this will help encourage your dog to repeat desired behaviors.

An example of negative reinforcement being used correctly can be found in one method of teaching a dog to sit. Using positive reinforcement, you can lure your dog into a sit by holding a treat above his head, which should make him set his hind end down in order to look up toward the treat. To further encourage your dog to sit, you can apply gentle pressure with your hand just above his hips. You should never push hard on his hips, as this can be painful and can be interpreted as a punishment. Gentle pressure is all that is needed. When your dog begins to sit down, remove the pressure immediately, letting him know that he did the right thing. At this point, the dog can also be rewarded with the treat. As you can see, negative reinforcement is nothing to fear and is quite helpful in many situations. Most owners use negative reinforcement during leash training without even realizing it.

Punishments

Punishments are used to discourage a dog from repeating a behavior in the future, which differentiates them from negative reinforcers. As previously mentioned, punishments should be quite mild, and even a sharp noise can be an effective punishment without any long-lasting negative effects on your dog's personality or behavior. For example, if you catch your dog digging in the garden, you might tell him 'No!' or clap your hands together to distract him. Your response obviously doesn't hurt him, but the noise is unpleasant enough that with repetition, he's less likely to repeat the undesirable behavior again.

Though punishments are a necessary part of dog training, it's essential that you never react with harsh or violent behavior. Never hit, kick, or scream at your dog. This won't teach him anything, and he may, in fact, lash out in fear if he feels that he needs to protect himself from you. Punishments should never leave lasting mental trauma or cause physical harm. Loud noises, verbal corrections, or even sprays of water are typically the harshest punishments that should be used. Even in cases of fighting and aggression, physically assaulting your dog is never acceptable.

Essential Commands

Doberman Pinschers are an intelligent breed that can learn nearly anything you wish to teach them. Depending on what you plan to do with your new dog, he may need to learn specific commands to succeed. However, there are a few basic commands that can be considered essential, no matter what your dog will be when he grows up. These essential commands will give your dog a basic education that can be built on as he progresses in his training. Whether you have a future show ring star or hiking buddy, it's crucial for your dog to learn how to recognize his own name, come when called, and walk politely on the leash. Once your Doberman has a good command of the basics, you can begin teaching him sport-specific commands or fun and interesting tricks.

Name Recognition

Unless you've brought home an adult Doberman and plan on keeping his given name, you'll likely need to teach your new dog to recognize his new name. Even some adult dogs don't have enough training in name recognition, so it's best to start from the beginning, no matter how much training your dog had in his previous home. This is a foundational skill that will be used for the rest of your dog's life, so it's important to start as soon as you bring your new Doberman Pinscher home.

For this exercise, it can be helpful to have your Doberman on a leash, especially if he's not particularly food driven or if he's easily distracted by his surroundings. To begin, say your dog's name and immediately hand him a reward, such as a training treat or piece of kibble. Repeat the process a few times, and be sure to reward him each time you say his name. Name recognition sessions should be short and repeated frequently, especially for the first few days after bringing your new dog home. With repetition, your dog will understand that when he hears his name, he should give you his attention as there may be something delicious in it for him.

Sit

The sit command is one of the easiest commands for a dog to learn, so most owners choose to teach it after name recognition. This command is particularly useful in many situations, such as asking your dog to sit and wait politely for his dinner or while you attach his leash before a walk. If you plan on competing with your Doberman, the sit command is also a required task in a variety of dog sports.

It's best to teach your Doberman Pinscher to sit while he is wearing a collar and leash, so he is unable to walk away from you if he gets distracted or loses interest. As mentioned in a previous section, you can use a combination of positive and negative reinforcement, or you can use positive reinforcement alone. Both methods will get results, but some dogs learn better one way over the other, so use your best judgment about what will work for your dog.

To use positive reinforcement alone, lure your dog into a sitting position by holding a treat just above his head. It should be out of reach, but not high enough that he feels that he needs to jump after it or stand up. Though he may be confused at first, most dogs understand quickly that sitting will put them in a better position to look up at the treat. The moment your Doberman's hind end touches the ground, give him the treat and praise him. It's helpful to introduce the motion a few times before using a verbal command, but with repetition, your dog will begin to connect the command 'sit' with this newly learned behavior.

*Photo Courtesy
of Rebecca Menapace and Joe Gross*

HELPFUL TIP
Doberman Personality

Dobermans tend to have a reputation for being aggressive and protective, but Doberman personalities can span a wide range of possibilities. Early and consistent training is an important step toward making sure that your Doberman doesn't develop troubling behavior problems such as aggression and dominance. With consistent training, even rescue dogs with behavior issues can become well adjusted. Dobermans are a highly intelligent breed, which often means that they learn quickly with good training.

If you'd like to use negative reinforcement to further encourage your dog to perform the correct behavior, there are two ways to do so. One way is to put gentle downward pressure on your dog's hips with one hand while luring him with the treat with the other hand. Once your dog's hind end moves down, release the pressure, and then reward him once his hind end touches the ground. Some trainers also teach the sit command by using gentle upward pressure on the leash to encourage the dog to sit and look up toward the treat. As before, once the dog sits, the pressure is removed immediately. Remember, timing is an important aspect of using negative reinforcement in dog training, so you need to release the pressure the moment your dog begins to perform the desired behavior.

Lie Down

Lie down is another easy-to-teach command that is useful in many everyday situations. Whether you want your Doberman Pinscher to rest calmly while you have coffee with friends at a local café or you need him to lie down for examination at the vet, it's a versatile skill for your dog to know. This command is also required knowledge for many different dog sports.

Many trainers choose to build upon the sit command to teach the lie down command, but others choose to teach it without referencing the sit. The method you choose will depend on your own training philosophy and what works best for your dog. Luring is typically the most common way to teach a dog to lie down. To begin, ask your dog to sit. From there, lure your dog to the ground by moving a treat down and slightly forward. At first, your dog may try to stand up or bend his head down to reach the treat. If he doesn't lie down right away, return him to the starting position and try again. Once his elbows touch the ground, reward him immediately.

You can also incorporate negative reinforcement into your training session if you so choose. While luring the dog with the treat, apply gentle downward pressure to encourage him to lie down. If your dog stiffens or does not move away from the pressure, simply hold the pressure constant. Do not increase the pressure or pull your dog into the down position. Be patient and your dog will eventually figure out what you're asking. At first, you may need to release the pressure the moment he begins to move downward, but with practice, you can relieve the pressure when he's lying down with his elbows touching the ground.

Stay

The stay command is crucial for any dog, whether he is an active companion or competitive sport dog. Using this command, you can teach your Doberman patience and respect. Plus, the stay command is required knowledge in several dog sports. Before you begin teaching this command, it's important to note that many trainers differentiate between a stay command and a wait command. Stay is generally used for longer periods of time, and the handler usually returns to the same position he or she started in before releasing the dog. The wait command is more temporary and is used for situations like waiting for breakfast or waiting for a recall command.

The stay can be performed in any position, but to begin with, you should choose the position your Doberman is most comfortable in. Once he understands the command in one position, you can move on to the others. Ask your dog to assume the desired position, such as standing, sitting, or lying down. Once he's in position, give him the wait or stay command and hesitate just a moment before giving him a reward. If your dog moves out of position before you reward and release him, simply move him back to where he was and try again. As your Doberman progresses in his training, you can try stepping back for a moment before returning to reward him. With regular training sessions, you can begin increasing the duration of the stays as well as the distance between you and your dog. For more advanced dogs, you can also add distractions like tossing treats on the floor, rolling a ball across the room, or stepping out of his line of sight.

Recall

The recall command is crucial for every dog, and it could even save your dog's life someday. A dog with a solid recall should drop everything and return to his owner on command, regardless of what's happening around him. Your dog should be able to perform this command anywhere, so be sure to practice in new places frequently.

To teach your dog to come when called, it's helpful to have an additional handler, so ask your friends or family members to assist if possible. Start in a quiet area such as your home or backyard. The fewer distractions the better during the early stages of training. If you're working outside, make sure it's an enclosed area or you're using a long leash. Ask your helper to hold your dog while you walk some distance away.

Gain your dog's attention by calling his name and give a verbal command such as 'Come!' or 'Come here!' and pat your legs or clap your hands to get your dog excited. Once you've given the command, your helper can release your dog, and he should run to meet you. When your Doberman reaches you, be sure to praise him enthusiastically and give him treats. Now that the dog is with you, you can hold him while your helper calls him back. This game can be played back and forth several times but be sure to quit before your dog loses focus. Running between handlers and thinking about what to do can be exhausting for puppies, so keep your sessions short and repeat them frequently.

Off

The off command is most useful around the house when you need your Doberman Pinscher to move off the furniture when asked. This command is sometimes confusing for owners who don't differentiate between the commands for getting off the sofa and lying down. If you use the word 'down' to ask your dog to lie down, it's important to use a different command such as 'off' to ask him to move off the furniture. The specific words don't matter, but you must be consistent in their usage.

Teaching your dog this command is easy, but you have the option of using positive reinforcement alone or a combination of positive and negative reinforcement. It's important to use caution with negative reinforcement with dogs that respond badly to pressure or have resource guarding issues. Safety should always be your priority.

To use positive reinforcement only, you'll want to lure your Doberman off the furniture using his favorite treat. As he begins to move toward the floor, give him the verbal command of choice to start developing that association. Once all four of his paws are on the ground, you can reward him with the treat and lots of praise.

There are several methods you can use to add negative reinforcement. The first is to have your dog wear a collar and short leash around the house at all times until he understands the rules of the house. As you lure him off the sofa, you can add a bit of gentle pressure with the leash. Once your Doberman begins moving toward the edge of the sofa, release the pressure and continue to lure him. As he begins to understand what you want, you can keep the pressure on him longer until his feet are on the floor but be sure to remove the pressure as soon as he does what you want and reward him accordingly. You can also use this method using a collar and your hand if you don't want your dog to wear a leash at all times. However, some dogs

react badly to this method, especially those with resource guarding issues. They may try to bite your hand when pressure is applied to their collars, so use a leash or positive reinforcement only if your dog is like this. You can also try applying gentle pressure from behind with one hand while you lure the dog with the other, but again, use caution with dogs you don't know well or those with behavioral problems. If you do choose to keep a leash on your dog to help with training the off command, remember to remove it when you aren't able to supervise him. Left unattended, he may get tangled up or chew or swallow the leash.

Drop It

The drop it command is another skill that will be incredibly useful around your home as well as on your daily walks. If your Doberman Pinscher picks up something inappropriate, you can ask him to give it to you. The command is also helpful in preventing or correcting resource guarding behavior.

Never try to remove an object from your Doberman's mouth with your bare hands. He will likely clamp his jaws down and refuse to let go, and he may also try to snap at you. Instead, you want to make a trade. Offer him something of higher value than whatever he already has in his mouth. In some cases, you may want to use something more delicious than his usual training treats, such as meat or cheese. Offer your dog the treat but try to lure him away from the object so that you can grab it without the risk of him biting you or grabbing the object out of your hands. Be sure to give the verbal command so your dog can build the association. It's helpful to practice this with items that he's allowed to have, such as toys or chews. Once he drops the item and you can grab it, you can simply give it back and try again.

Leave It

Once you begin teaching your dog to leave it, you will likely find yourself using the drop it command less frequently. Whether you're taking a walk around the neighborhood or participating at a local dog show, you don't want your Doberman to get distracted by everything around you. In order to keep him focused and prevent him from grabbing unknown items off the ground, you need to teach him to leave it.

Again, the specific words you use aren't important. Many trainers use 'leave it' or 'walk away,' but you can use whatever works best for you. Keeping your Doberman on a leash is essential so that you can reinforce your request by preventing him from wandering off to investigate. When your dog gets distracted by an interesting smell or sight, give him the verbal command and wave a high-value treat in front of his face. Once he smells the treat, he'll likely refocus, and you can lure him a step or two away from the direction of the distraction before rewarding him. As he begins to understand, you can have him walk for longer distances before rewarding him for leaving the distraction alone.

Advanced Commands

As your Doberman Pinscher progresses in his training, you can begin increasing the level of challenge in his daily training sessions. Not only will this help him learn more, but it will keep the sessions fresh and interesting for him, while also engaging his mind and body more. If you want to show him in the future or compete in dog sports, you can start to teach him sport-specific commands. Trick training can also be a fun way to bond with your Doberman and stimulate his mind. The AKC also has a new Trick Dog class that you can compete in if you enjoy showing off your dog's skills. You can also simply increase the challenge of the commands your dog already knows. Try increasing the length of stays or the distance of your recalls. You can also start practicing in areas with more distractions, such as busier parks or areas of town.

Regardless of what you choose to teach your Doberman Pinscher, it's important to keep your training sessions short to keep your dog engaged and interested in training. At first, you may need to keep it as short as three to five minutes to prevent your dog from losing focus. Going beyond what your dog's attention span can handle will only frustrate him and discourage him from engaging in future training sessions. If your dog doesn't seem to understand what you're asking, try asking him to perform a task he already knows a few times. This way, you can reward him and end on a good note. Then you can end the session and reflect on why he doesn't understand what you're asking. You can always return to the original task in a future session. Remember, you need to instill confidence in your dog, so be sure that he can feel good about himself and his abilities after every training session.

CHAPTER 13
The Doberman Pinscher for Work and Sport

"Dobermans are incredibly intelligent and do well in performance events. There are many to choose from: Obedience, Rally, Barn hunt, Dock diving, and many more."

PAMELA DEHETRE
Pamelot, Reg.

The Doberman Pinscher and Dog Sports

Doberman Pinschers are incredible athletes capable of succeeding in a variety of sports and types of work. Their athleticism combined with their intelligence means you'll have a capable partner no matter what you choose to do with your new dog. However, the benefits of working or competing with your dog go both ways. Not only will you have the partner of your dreams, but your dog will have ample physical and mental exercise to keep him interested and active.

Doberman Pinschers were originally bred as protectors, but after decades of breeding for specific purposes, the breed is now an all-around athlete. No matter what modern dog sport competition you attend, you're bound to see at least one Doberman there.

Protection Sports

There is a common misconception that dogs who are trained for protection become aggressive or more prone to violence, but this simply isn't true. Protection sports require stable temperaments and level-headed decision making. Aggressive or mentally unstable dogs will not succeed. In order to compete in protection sports, dogs must be safe to handle among the general public and must only react aggressively when the situation calls for it, such as when the handler is under threat.

Though there are a variety of protection sports in which dogs may compete, Schutzhund is where Doberman Pinschers shine. Schutzhund, or IPO, is a German dog sport that was originally designed to test the abilities of the German Shepherd. The sport is still dominated by German Shepherds, but Doberman Pinschers are one of the most commonly seen breeds at these events.

Dogs that compete in IPO must pass a temperament test prior to competing in the three levels of difficulty. Once the dog's temperament has passed the test, the dog can move on to the three stages of Schutzhund: tracking, obedience, and bitework. In the first stage, dogs must find two articles of clothing along a 600-to-900-foot track. The articles must be in place for at least 20 minutes prior to the dog's arrival and must be laid in place by the handler. Dogs then have 15 minutes to find the articles. Then, the dogs move on to obedience, where they must perform a pattern of commands memorized by the handler. The final stage of IPO is protection, where the dog must combine obedience with courage to succeed. Here, the dog's bitework will be tested. A bad guy, or helper, is assigned to threaten the handler, and the dog must be willing to bite when necessary. He must also let go on command. IPO is a difficult sport, and not all dogs have what it takes to succeed. But purpose bred Dobermans are among the top athletes in the IPO world.

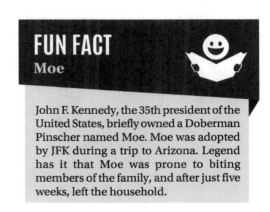

FUN FACT
Moe

John F. Kennedy, the 35th president of the United States, briefly owned a Doberman Pinscher named Moe. Moe was adopted by JFK during a trip to Arizona. Legend has it that Moe was prone to biting members of the family, and after just five weeks, left the household.

Therapy and Service Dogs

The gentle demeanor and incredible intelligence of the Doberman Pinscher are the perfect combination for therapy and service dogs. If you're not familiar, therapy dogs are dogs that volunteer in stressful environments like schools, nursing homes, and hospitals to put the residents at ease. Service dogs, on the other hand, are specially trained to perform specific tasks to aid their handler, who generally has a disability. Service dogs are allowed to accompany their handler everywhere, while therapy dogs do not have the same access. Therapy dogs can, however, earn a Therapy Dog title from the American Kennel Club.

If you are interested in training your Doberman Pinscher to become a therapy or service dog, it's important to discuss this with the breeder prior to committing to a puppy or adult dog. Not all dogs are capable of being successful therapy or service dogs, so you want to make sure you're getting a dog with the right temperament.

Obedience

If you're looking for a sport to test your training skills, obedience might be right up your alley. Obedience demonstrates your Doberman Pinscher's usefulness as a companion. The competition exhibits dogs' abilities to behave themselves and obey the commands of their handlers, even in the stressful and distracting environment of a dog show. Accuracy and precision are key.

The commands you'll need to teach your Doberman will vary according to the level of competition. Lower levels of obedience are performed on leash, while more advanced levels are done off leash. Dogs are generally asked to sit, lie down, stay, heel, jump over obstacles, come when called, and retrieve dumbbells. These may seem easy, but they are combined in ways that challenge competitors and test their abilities.

If you're looking for a less formal competition, consider rally. It takes the same skills needed to succeed in obedience but applies them in a manner that mimics real life. Instead of commands being called out by judges, in rally, dogs and their handlers must navigate a course with signs indicating which task is required in that location. The course may be completed at each team's desired speed. Like obedience, there are varying levels of difficulty, with some being performed off leash. Some classes also have jumps.

Agility

Doberman Pinschers are athletic dogs that excel in agility. If you're not familiar with this exciting, high-speed event, dogs must follow the direction of their handlers to complete an obstacle course as quickly and accurately as possible. There is a time limit called the standard course time, and if the dog exceeds the standard course time, time faults are incurred. Penalties may also be incurred if dogs knock down bars off jumps, refuse obstacles, or go off course. The fastest time with the fewest penalties wins. The competition is divided by dogs' heights to ensure that it's fair. Bigger breeds like Dobermans will not be competing with smaller breeds such as Papillons. The entire course is completed off leash, and touching the dog or the obstacles is forbidden. As such, agility requires a strong bond between dog and handler as well as excellent communication.

The obstacles included in an agility course will vary according to the organization in charge of the competition. Some of the most common obstacles include an A-frame, which is simply a triangular-shaped obstacle made of two ramps with a hinge in the middle. It's normally raised to between five and six feet. Other obstacles include a dog walk, which is a raised plank approximately 12 feet in length with ramps on either end. There is also a seesaw, which is a 10-to-12-foot plank that pivots on an off-center fulcrum. The fulcrum is off-center so that the same side always returns to the ground once the dog has moved on from the obstacle, preparing the course for the next dog. There are also tunnels, some of which have one side that is collapsed, which requires dogs to push their way through, and a variety of jumps, including horizontal bars, hoops, and panels. Jumps are adjusted according to the different size classes, so small dogs will never have to jump the same height as large dogs. Weave poles are another exciting obstacle that require dogs to weave between five and twelve upright poles set in a line. A pause table or box may also be present. This obstacle is a raised table or taped off square where dogs are required to sit or lie down for around five seconds. Depending on the organization in charge, there may be more obstacles, but these are the most commonly encountered.

*Photo Courtesy
of Tayla Jade*

Fast CAT

One of AKC's newest events is Fast CAT, which stands for Fast Coursing Ability Test. It's a timed 100-yard dash where dogs run one at a time after a lure. It's similar to lure coursing for sighthounds, but it's a shorter distance designed for dogs of all breeds. There is little training needed to compete, as the competition relies on a dog's natural instinct to pursue prey.

Typically, the event requires two handlers—one to release the dog at the start line and one to catch him at the finish line. Depending on the club, dogs may compete for the fastest time for a certain size, but typically dogs are only competing directly against their own breed. The AKC publishes a list of the Top 20 Fastest Dogs by Breed on their website.

Dock Diving

If your Doberman Pinscher loves water, you might consider getting involved with dock diving. As the name implies, dogs dive off a dock, and the competition is judged by how far each is able to leap into the water. To maximize the distance, handlers give the dogs a running start and toss a floating toy out over the water. The dog covering the most distance wins.

Canicross/Bikejoring/Skijoring

If you want to be as active as your dog, consider getting into one of the joring sports such as canicross or bikejoring. These sports originally began in Europe as a way of keeping sled dogs fit during their off-season, but it has risen in popularity among owners of all breeds. In canicross, owners may

compete with one or two dogs at a time. The dogs are outfitted in special harnesses designed for pulling and mushing. They are connected to a waist harness worn by the handler with a bungee leash to help reduce impact on both dog and runner. The teams of handlers and dogs then compete against each other the same as any other foot race. Distances may vary, but the fast team wins.

Bikejoring is similar to canicross, but the dog's leash is attached to a mountain bike or kick bike instead of a waist harness. The dog or dogs run ahead of the bike, and the race proceeds the same as any other bike race. Skijoring is basically the same as the other two sports but takes place only in winter. The handler wears cross country skis, and the dog is attached to the handler's waist harness.

Nosework

Nosework is a relatively new sport that is designed to simulate professional detection dogs. Competing dogs must search indoor or outdoor areas, including vehicles, to find items scented with birch, anise, or clove oil. Similar to professional detection dogs, dogs competing in nosework must signal to their handlers once they've found the scent. This is a great sport for dogs with mobility issues as the sport focuses on scenting ability rather than speed or athletic ability.

CHAPTER 14
Nutrition

"A balanced diet is key. Avoid fad diets and marketing ploys, such as grain-free unless your veterinarian has determined that your dog is in need of a restrictive diet. A high quality, premium dry kibble is normally best. If you have a picky eater you can always add warm water or a tablespoon of canned food to make it more palatable."

TRACY DOTY
Halo Dobermans

Photo Courtesy of Summer Satterlee

The Importance of a Balanced Diet

A balanced diet is essential for growing puppies, healthy adult Doberman Pinschers, and aging seniors alike. A diet lacking in certain nutrients can put any dog at risk of developing debilitating and even life-threatening health conditions. Although every dog, no matter the age, needs to be fed a balanced and nutritious diet, it's especially important for growing puppies. Without the right balance of fats, proteins, and carbohydrates, their growth may be stunted or altered. The effects of an unbalanced diet are not immediately visible, and you may not see the impact for several weeks or months. Depending on the type of nutritional imbalance you're dealing with, the effects could be permanent, so appropriate nutrition for your Doberman is key.

DOBERMANS IN FICTION
Elwood Doberman Jr.

Elwood Doberman Jr. is an early reader, published by WestBow Press, that follows the antics and adventures of a rebellious Doberman named Elwood. The spirited dog loves riding around town on his yellow bike and causing his parents anxiety. After a string of particularly frustrating missteps, Elwood's parents send him to West Pointer Academy in hopes of teaching him a lesson, but will Elwood learn to take responsibility for his actions? This heartwarming tale is written and illustrated by Mary Rhee who hopes that this story will entertain and inspire parents and children alike.

One of the most overlooked aspects of a properly balanced diet is portion control. Your Doberman needs not only the correct combination of nutrients in his diet but the proper number of calories as well. Obesity is a common health problem in dogs of all ages and can have a serious impact on your dog's overall health, so it's important to feed your dog the right sized portions to help him maintain a healthy weight. Portion sizes vary according to each dog's unique needs, so even dogs of the same age and lifestyle may need different size portions to compensate for their individual metabolisms. Puppies and active or working dogs will require far more calories than senior dogs or those that lead a more sedentary life. Additionally, different types of food have different caloric content, so your portion sizes should account for your dog's needs as well as the type of food you're giving him. If you're unsure of what portion size is best for your dog based on the type of food you feed, ask your veterinarian or consult a professional canine nutritionist.

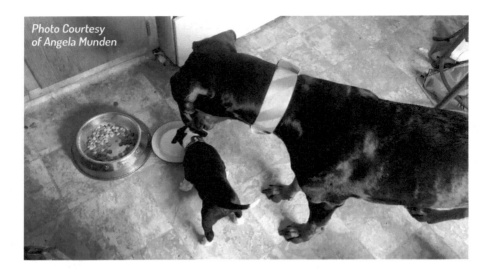

Photo Courtesy of Angela Munden

Basic Nutrition

Canine nutrition is an incredibly complex subject that even veterinary professionals often choose to learn only the basics of. Professional canine nutritionists study the way modern dogs are fed in order to improve the lives of our beloved pets and the performance of working and sport dogs. This section of the book covers the absolute basics of nutrition, so if you need advice on your Doberman Pinscher's diet or have questions concerning canine nutrition, it's best to ask a professional. Your veterinarian may be able to answer relatively simple nutrition questions, but it's unlikely that they'll have the knowledge required to answer more in-depth questions. If you need to seek the advice of a specialist, the American College of Veterinary Nutrition (ACVN) has a list of board-certified veterinary nutritionists on their website.

Proteins and Amino Acids

Amino acids and proteins share a close relationship as amino acids are the organic material needed to form proteins. As molecules of protein break down during the process of digestion, amino acids are the result. Your Doberman Pinscher's body then uses those amino acids to form different protein molecules in order to grow, maintain, and repair cells within the body. This is why canine diets should be high in protein. By some estimates,

131

it takes around 30 percent of your dog's daily protein intake to maintain the cells in his coat alone.

To form these various proteins, your dog has 20 amino acids within his body. Some are produced naturally, while others must be supplied by diet. The amino acids that must be supplied by your Doberman's diet are called essential amino acids because of their importance. If your dog's diet is lacking in these amino acids, his system will not be able to form certain proteins, which can negatively impact his growth and health.

The ten essential amino acids are:

- Arginine
- Histidine
- Isoleucine
- Leucine
- Lysine
- Methionine
- Phenylalanine
- Threonine
- Tryptophan
- Valine

Foods common in canine diets such as muscle meat, eggs, and dairy products are high in protein and provide your dog with the essential amino acids his body needs for protein synthesis. Few plants contain enough protein for a dog's body to function properly, so the amount of plant matter in your dog's diet should be low. Vegetarian and vegan diets are not biologically appropriate for any dog and should be avoided.

Fat and Fatty Acids

The most concentrated energy source in your Doberman Pinscher's diet is fat. Fats provide your dog's body with a condensed source of calories and fatty acids, which are the building blocks for various substances responsible for cell growth and maintenance within the body. Fatty acids are similar to amino acids, but fewer are required to be included in a balanced diet. Fats also help with the absorption of fat-soluble vitamins like vitamins A, D, E, and K. Many dogs also find diets high in fat to be more palatable, so they may appeal more to picky eaters.

The essential fatty acids are:

- Arachidonic acid
- Linoleic acid
- Linolenic acid

You've probably seen various dog foods and supplements touting the benefits of omega-3 and omega-6 fatty acids. In your Doberman Pinscher's diet, omega-3 fatty acids are provided by linolenic acid, and omega-6 fatty acids are provided by linoleic acid. A proper balance of omega-3 and omega-6 fatty acids is required. More omega-6 fatty acids are required than omega-3, usually at a recommended ratio of 4:1.

Carbohydrates

Carbohydrates are a somewhat controversial subject in the world of canine nutrition. While carbohydrates do provide dogs with energy, there are often more efficient sources of energy available. Carbs are not a necessary requirement for dogs, and many choose to avoid feeding their dogs grains and carb-heavy vegetables. Most kibbles tend to use carbohydrates as fillers to help reduce the cost of the product. Plenty of homemade diets also include high quantities of carbs, and most dogs tolerate it just fine. As with any diet, some dogs have a higher tolerance for carbs than others, so the carbohydrates included in your Doberman Pinscher's diet will vary according to his individual needs.

In the digestive system, carbohydrates are broken down into glucose, which provides your dog's body with energy. Some carbohydrates, especially vegetables, also provide additional nutrients such as antioxidants, minerals, and phytochemicals. They're also a great source of dietary fiber, but starchy carbohydrates will need to be cooked or blended in order to be fully digestible.

Feeding Dogs at Different Life Stages

As your Doberman Pinscher's needs change throughout his lifetime, his nutritional needs will change accordingly, and you'll need to adjust his diet to adapt. As you browse your local pet store's food shelves, you may notice various dog foods labeled for use with dogs of 'all life stages.' This means that these foods have been formulated using the Association of American Feed Control Officials' (AAFCO) nutritional standards, so they are nutritionally balanced, but they may or may not be appropriate for all dogs in all life stages.

Remember, when you bring your Doberman Pinscher home as a puppy, he's going to need a higher number of calories and a specific balance of vitamins and minerals in order to grow and develop properly. As an adult dog, his nutritional needs will vary according to his lifestyle. A working dog will obviously require more calories and a potentially different diet than the average pet dog. Senior dogs may require a reduced calorie content and different nutrients to help them cope with the struggles of aging.

Unaltered dogs will also have different nutritional needs than those that have been spayed or neutered. Additionally, pregnant and lactating dogs will require a specific diet to help them maintain their own health while also providing nutrients to their growing puppies. In all of these scenarios, a food formulated for all life stages would be fine, but it wouldn't provide each dog with the ideal ratios of nutrients he or she needs to thrive in their specific situations.

So, while food formulated for dogs of all life stages is technically a balanced diet, it may not be ideal for your Doberman Pinscher's specific needs. Even if you have multiple dogs in your home, you may need to tailor each dog's diet and portion size to its own individual needs at a specific stage in life.

Different Types of Commercial Food

When most dog owners think of commercial dog food, they think of kibble. It's by far the most popular and widely available kind of dog food. Owners love it because it's easy to find, relatively inexpensive, and convenient to feed. There is also a nearly endless variety of formulas designed for dogs of any age, size, or health status. If your Doberman has heart disease, food allergies, or is an active working dog, you should be able to find a kibble formulated for his specific needs. Kibble is made with a wide variety of ingredients. Some kibble contains grain, while other kibble products are grain-free. You can find different protein options such as beef, lamb, or chicken, as well as novel proteins like kangaroo and pork.

Kibble is the most popular type of commercial dog food because it's easy to feed, even if you have little to no experience with canine nutrition. In the United States, commercial dog foods are formulated to adhere to AAFCO standards of

FUN FACT
What is B.A.R.F.?

B.A.R.F. stands for "Biologically Appropriate Raw Food" and is a dog feeding program developed by veterinarian and nutritionist Dr. Ian Billinghurst. This raw meat diet has gained popularity among Doberman owners in recent years and claims to offer benefits for your pet's coat, skin, teeth, and energy levels. But it also comes with its share of risks. Critics of the diet cite concerns about bacteria in raw meat, an unbalanced diet from prolonged use, and risks of internal puncture or tooth breakage from bones. Be sure to speak with your veterinarian before switching to an experimental diet for your Doberman.

nutrition, so you don't need to worry about feeding your dog an unbalanced diet. Kibble also comes in a range of prices to suit every budget. Prescription kibble, however, tends to be quite expensive and may only be available from your veterinarian.

For dogs with food sensitivities or allergies, some of the most common carbohydrates in commercial dog food are often the cause of the reaction: corn, wheat, and soy. This is why many owners are switching their dogs to grain-free diets, where the more traditional grains are replaced by starchy vegetables like peas and potatoes. It's worth mentioning that some veterinarians do not recommend grain-free kibble as there may be a correlation between grain-free kibble and the development of dilated cardiomyopathy (DCM). The link has not yet been proven, and some vets would prefer to err on the side of caution until more research can reveal a more definitive conclusion. If you have any questions regarding your Doberman's food and its potential link to DCM, ask your veterinarian or a veterinary nutritionist.

Another popular commercial food is canned dog food, which is ideal for many older dogs or finicky eaters. Canned food has a soft consistency and tends to be more palatable than kibble, so it's a good choice for dogs who would prefer not to eat kibble or those that need to gain a little weight. Like kibble, it comes in a wide range of formulas to suit almost any dog. It also has a higher moisture content than kibble, so it's helpful for dogs that don't drink enough water on their own. Canned food is often more calorie dense than kibble, so it's important to make sure you're giving your dog properly sized portions. Canned food tends to stick to dogs' teeth more than kibble, so you may need to consider more intensive dental care such as daily brushing or more frequent professional cleaning.

A newer option among commercial diets is fresh-cooked dog food, which is found in the refrigerated section of your local pet or grocery store. It's often packaged in rolls, and portions can be sliced off as needed and returned to the fridge for storage. Commercial fresh-cooked diets are the ideal diet for owners who want to provide their dogs with the nutrition of a homecooked meal but are unwilling or unable to properly balance and cook their dog's food themselves. Fresh food does generally cost more than most brands of kibble or canned food, but it's a good compromise for owners who aren't quite ready to prepare their dog's meals at home.

An increasing number of dog owners are educating themselves about canine nutrition and seek to feed their dogs a biologically appropriate diet, but they often don't have the time or knowledge necessary to make their dog's food themselves. Commercial raw diets are intended to provide these types of owners with a balanced and species-appropriate diet, without the hard work of a homemade diet. You can generally find commercial raw dog food in the freezer section of your local pet store. It's available in a variety of proteins and serving sizes. The food is generally available in quick-thawing pellets, nuggets, or patties to suit dogs of every size. It's made of a nutritionally balanced blend of meat, bones, organs, and fruits and vegetables. Raw foods tend to be the most expensive commercially available canine diet, especially for larger dogs, so some budget-conscious choose to feed their dogs half kibble and half raw.

Homemade Diets

Homemade diets are the dog food of choice for owners interested in having full control over what their Doberman Pinscher eats. However, making your dog's food requires a significant time commitment and can be more expensive than a commercial diet depending on the ingredients you use and their availability where you live. It's your responsibility to make sure the homemade diet you make for your Doberman is nutritionally balanced. As previously mentioned, nutritional imbalances typically aren't apparent for some time, and it is possible to permanently damage your Doberman's health, especially if he's still growing.

If you're not sure that your grasp of canine nutrition is enough to properly balance your Doberman Pinscher's food, you should seek the advice of a canine nutritionist. The American College of Veterinary Nutrition (ACVN) publishes a list on their website of the board-certified veterinary nutritionists located all over the world. Though some nutritionists will formulate diets according to AAFCO, many follow the recommendations of the National Research Council (NRC). This is the best way to make sure you're feeding your Doberman a diet suited to his general health, food sensitivities, and activity level while also keeping in mind ingredient availability and any budget concerns.

Homemade raw diets are the most common type of dog food made at home and can usually be put into one of two categories: Prey Model Raw (PRM) or Biologically Appropriate Raw Food (BARF). PMR diets simulate the diet of wild dogs and use the approximate percentages of meat, bone, and organ contained in prey animals. These diets usually follow a rough guideline of 80% muscle meat, 10% bone, and 10% organ. Some PMR diets may allow for a small percentage of fruits and vegetables, but many do not. BARF diets are similar to PMR diets but generally allow for more vegetables and the addition of starchy carbs such as oats, barley, or potato. Both PMR and BARF feeders also supplement their dogs' diets with fermented fish stock, bone broth, or goat milk to provide additional nutrients. Regardless of the type of raw diet, it's important to note that many of these percentage-based diets are lacking in critical nutrients such as zinc, manganese, and vitamin E. However, with the help of a canine nutritionist, you should be able to formulate a balanced raw recipe for your Doberman Pinscher.

Cooked diets are another type of homemade dog food that are popular among owners who want to make their own food but are unable or unwilling to work with raw food. Families with members who are immunocompromised are generally recommended to choose a cooked diet for their dogs over raw so as not to expose their family to any potential pathogens that may be contained in the raw ingredients. For cooked diets, the contents are often the same as raw diets, but the ingredients are usually baked or boiled prior to feeding. Many cooked diets also contain grains such as barley or rice. As with raw diets, many owners who feed homecooked dog food supplement with vitamin mixtures, kelp, and dairy products. Calcium is usually provided with the use of ground eggshells, seaweed calcium, or a calcium supplement rather than bones. This is because cooked bones can splinter and injure your dog, whereas raw bones are safer and more digestible.

However, care must be taken when feeding your dog homemade diets, especially those that include bones. Raw bones do not shatter in the same manner as cooked bones, but weight-bearing bones, such as those in the legs of livestock, may be too hard and may put your dog at risk of chipping or cracking a tooth. Some dogs are able to use these types of bones as recreational chews, but heavy chewers may risk dental damage. Always monitor your dog when giving him any type of bone so that you can intervene if needed. Some dogs need practice with bones or large chunks of food to learn that they cannot gulp large items. A small percentage of dogs never learn to chew their food correctly and must be prevented from attempting to swallow large chunks of food whole. With these types of dogs, it's usually recommended to grind their food or provide them with chunks that are large enough they can't possibly try to swallow them whole.

Remember, when feeding your Doberman Pinscher a homemade diet, it's solely your responsibility to make sure it's nutritionally balanced and safe to feed. Part of this safety involves keeping your human family safe. Very few raw feeders experience any type of illness associated with the handling of raw meat, but it's still important to follow proper hygiene practices. Always clean your prep area as you would if you were preparing meat to be cooked for your family, and consider restricting your dog's access to your home while he's eating. Some dogs like to take their food to a different area of the house to eat, and dragging raw meat around the house can spread potentially dangerous pathogens. Rather than allowing your dog to eat his meals on the carpet or furniture, consider feeding him outside or in his kennel. Some owners may also choose to wipe down their dog's paws and face after meals to help keep them clean and prevent them from spreading germs around the home.

Photo Courtesy of Lisa Abele

Weight Management

Research performed by the Association of Pet Obesity Prevention suggests that approximately 52 percent of adult dogs are considered to be overweight or obese. About 90% of owners of obese dogs do not recognize that their dogs weigh more than they should. Obesity can cause serious health problems and dramatically affect your Doberman Pinscher's ability to enjoy his life. Though you may be tempted to give your beloved dog a treat every time he asks for one, you need to be responsible enough to say no. Keeping a close eye on your dog's weight at home is important, but you may not be able to recognize an unhealthy weight when you see it. When you take your Doberman in for his regular checkups, be sure to ask your veterinarian if your dog is at a healthy weight, and if not, what should be done about it. Though breed standards have a suggested weight range for each breed, not all individuals will be at a healthy weight even if they're within range. A healthy weight is determined according to each individual dog's physical size. Even two Dobermans who weigh the same may not both be at a healthy weight due to differences in height and frame size.

One of the most important factors in weight management is portion size. Even if you're feeding your Doberman a proper amount of food for

Photo Courtesy
of Shannon Westmoreland

breakfast and dinner, you need to remember to include his edible chews and training treats into your calculations. You might be able to forget about the handful of treats you use in your daily training session, but your dog's waistline may be less forgiving. If your dog needs to lose weight and is on a restricted diet, consider swapping some of his high calorie treats for healthier options like vegetables. Fruit may also be used but sparingly due to the high sugar content.

Another important factor of weight control is physical activity. The more your Doberman Pinscher does during his day, the more he'll be able to eat. If your dog needs to lose weight and you're not willing to cut his portion sizes, you need to be exercising him more. Increased physical exercise will also keep him busy and help prevent him from developing boredom-induced bad behaviors like digging or chewing.

Food Allergies and Intolerances

After you've decided what type of food you want to feed your Doberman Pinscher, your work is not yet done. You'll need to monitor your dog to make sure that he's tolerating the food well. Approximately ten percent of all allergies in dogs are food allergies, so even though the rate is low, you still need to be diligent. Allergic reactions are responses by your dog's immune system to certain proteins in his diet, while intolerances are usually less severe. They may appear as simple digestive upset or the inability to fully digest certain diet ingredients. Generalized itching is one of the most common symptoms of food allergies, but your dog may also experience ear or skin infections, vomiting, or diarrhea. Common ingredients that can cause allergic reactions or digestive upset include chicken, beef, lamb, soy, wheat, and corn.

Diagnosing a food allergy is not a simple process, so if you suspect your Doberman Pinscher may be allergic to an ingredient in his food, you'll need to be patient while you and your vet determine which ingredient is the cause. Allergy tests are possible, but the results aren't always reliable. Most vets will instead recommend an elimination diet, performed over several weeks or months. With an elimination diet, your dog will be placed on a food containing a novel protein like salmon or kangaroo. Few dogs are allergic to novel proteins, so it's the best place to start. Once your dog seems to be doing well on his new food, you can begin introducing individual ingredients one at a time to see if there is a reaction. Each additional protein should be fed for several weeks at a time before moving on to the next to allow for enough time for a reaction to develop.

If the specific protein causing your dog's reaction cannot be pinpointed, your vet may suggest a hypoallergenic diet. Hypoallergenic diets are usually available by prescription only and are formulated using hydrolyzed proteins. Hydrolyzed proteins are proteins that are broken down into sizes small enough that they won't set off the immune system. These types of diets are usually quite expensive, so most owners rely on them only as a last resort.

Working and Sport Dog Nutrition

Doberman Pinschers that are working dogs or are heavily involved in dog sports will require different nutrition than a dog that lives a more casual lifestyle. Canine athletes require a much higher number of calories each day than the average pet, sometimes as much as 1.5 to 2.5 times more. Dogs working in particularly hot or cold climates will require even more, as they will burn extra calories to regulate their internal temperatures. Many canine athletes will also require a higher fat and protein content, but care should be taken to avoid feeding too much fat as it can cause pancreatitis and digestive upset. Feeding immediately before or after strenuous exercise should also be avoided. Most experts recommend resting for an hour between food and exercise.

The specific ratio of proteins, fats, and carbohydrates required by the working or sport dog will vary according to each dog's metabolism and the type of work they do. Sprint athletes, such as those involved in agility and protection sports, work in short, intense bursts. They don't usually need a large increase in calories and can thrive on a high-quality diet containing around 300 to 400 calories per cup. The dry matter content of carbohydrates should be between 40% and 50%. The dry matter fats should be below 15%, and protein should equal about 25%.

Remember, dry matter measuring is the most accurate method of measuring the ingredients in dog food as moisture content varies by brand. Dry matter measurements are taken once all moisture has been removed. You can find the dry matter content of your dog food somewhere on its packaging. This information will also be available on the manufacturer's website.

For dogs that need to do intense physical activity for longer periods of time, up to a few hours, an increase in fat is recommended, usually a dry matter content of about 30% to 35%. Dogs involved in true endurance sports will require the most nutrient-dense food available. Food containing 500 to 600 calories per cup and between 30% and 35% each of fat, protein, and carbs is recommended. Endurance athletes will need a significantly higher number of calories than the average pet dog.

Working dog nutrition is a complicated matter, so if you have any questions about feeding your canine athlete, contact a veterinary nutritionist.

There are many who specialize in working and sport dog diets, so they'll be especially helpful in finding the right diet to suit your Doberman Pinscher's nutrition needs.

It should also be noted that working and sport dogs require far more water than less active dogs. By some estimates, canine athletes may consume as much as 10 to 20 times more water. Remember, if your dog is working in warm weather, he's going to require more water than usual, so make sure your Doberman has access to fresh drinking water when he needs it. Though it's not recommended to ever limit your dog's water intake, you should be careful about letting him fill his stomach with water during or after strenuous activities. A stomach full of water during exercise could lead to bloat, so you need to make sure your Doberman drinks frequently but doesn't fill his stomach.

CHAPTER 15
Physical and Mental Exercise

"Your Doberman will be a happy well balanced dog if he is stimulated both physically and mentally. At a minimum, your Doberman will need at least two outings per day. A long walk and a game of fetch, in addition to bathroom outings can suffice as long as you are also challenging him mentally. A bored dog can become a destructive dog."

TRACY DOTY
Halo Dobermans

Photo Courtesy
of Savannah McCorkle

The Importance of Physical Exercise

The benefits of providing your Doberman Pinscher with adequate physical activity are innumerable, but one of the greatest benefits of exercise is its role in helping your dog maintain a healthy weight. Along with portion control, daily physical exercise will help prevent your Doberman from becoming overweight or obese. Obesity is one of the most common health problems faced by adult dogs, and affected dogs are at risk of developing arthritis, diabetes, and heart disease. To keep your dog as healthy as possible, be sure to provide him with physical activity each and every day.

Physical exercise is also an essential part of preventing behavioral problems caused by boredom. Most forms of physical activity will also provide your Doberman Pinscher with mental stimulation, and it helps to keep your dog's mind as fit as his body. Even a brisk walk around your neighborhood or hike at your local trailhead will provide your dog with new sights and smells that he wouldn't get to experience lying around at home all day. If you don't regularly provide your dog with these types of activities to exercise his mind and body, he will likely attempt to entertain himself around your home. Unfortunately, dogs tend to entertain themselves with destructive behavior like chewing, digging, or escaping your yard. Remember, a tired dog is more likely to be a well-behaved dog around the house.

It's important to note that there is no specified amount of physical exercise that you need to provide your dog with each day. The amount of time you spend exercising your Doberman Pinscher will depend on his age, physical fitness, energy level, and overall health. Particularly young and old dogs will usually have far less stamina than a healthy adult dog. Some health problems may also affect a dog's ability to exercise, so be sure to consult your vet if your dog has any serious health concerns before exercising him. For most healthy adult Dobermans, one to three hours of physical activity each day should be enough.

Your Doberman Pinscher's daily amount of exercise does

DOBERMANS IN FILM
Blackie

"Hugo", the award-winning 2011 film directed by Martin Scorsese, features a Doberman named Blackie, who stars alongside Sasha Baron Cohen as the train station officer attack dog. Blackie was trained on set by French trainer Mathilde de Cagny. On the movie set, Blackie was nicknamed "Citizen Canine". Scorsese encouraged fans to vote for Blackie as a write-in after the dog was snubbed for the first annual Golden Collar Awards.

not need to happen all at once. If you intend to exercise your dog for three hours each day, this doesn't mean you need to take him for a three-hour walk each morning before work. That three hours may include any combination of walking, hiking, running, training, or even playing around with other dogs or humans. Feel free to spread that time throughout the day. If you only have time for a 30-minute walk before work, you can spend more time exercising your dog when you get home in the evening. Remember, young and old dogs do not have much stamina and will typically do best with shorter, more frequent activities. Healthy adult dogs, on the other hand, may gladly accompany you on a day-long hike if that's how you spend your time. However you choose to exercise your Doberman, most behaviorists will recommend exercising your dog for as long as possible in the morning if you are away for a typical 8-hour workday. This way, your dog will be more willing to sleep and relax while you're at work.

To provide your Doberman Pinscher with the most physical and mental exercise, you should consider trying different activities throughout the week. A variety of activities will help keep your dog active and interested in working with you. A daily walk around the neighborhood is certainly better than nothing, but you may find that you and your Doberman will get bored walking the same route each and every day. Doberman Pinschers love spending time with their people, so the more activities you can include your dog in, the better. Whether you're going hiking, mountain biking, or paddle boarding, your Doberman would be happy to join you. Training classes are also a great way to exercise your dog and improve your bond with him. Basic obedience classes are a great place to start, but don't be afraid to try new sports such

*Photo Courtesy
of Dara and Woody Spencer*

as agility, dock diving, or even barn hunt. Even if you don't consider yourself to be a 'dog sport person,' a training class might be a fun opportunity to learn something new and keep you both active.

Exercising Puppies

It's important to use caution when exercising your Doberman Pinscher puppy before around 18 months of age. Strenuous physical exercise can permanently damage a puppy's developing body if he is pushed too hard. Before the growth plates are fully closed, usually around 18 months of age, the risk of joint damage is high. This doesn't mean you should avoid exercising your Doberman puppy, but you do need to be cautious about the length and difficulty of exercise sessions.

Even training sessions should be kept short, not only for the puppy's limited attention span but also for the safety of his growing body. Training sessions between five and fifteen minutes in length are recommended, but you should adjust according to your Doberman puppy's individual needs. You can repeat these training sessions throughout the day, but you need to stop each session before your puppy begins to get tired or distracted. For example, if you note that your puppy seems to get tired or loses focus at around five minutes into every training session, you should try to quit at around three or four minutes. This way, your puppy will not associate exhaustion or frustration with your lessons, and he'll be more willing to participate in the next one. If the training session is particularly strenuous, either physically or mentally, you need to keep the sessions even shorter than usual.

There are some socialization and training programs, such as Puppy Culture, that suggest that a puppy should be exercised for no more than five minutes for every month of the puppy's age. For example, with these guidelines, a three-month-old puppy would be allowed no more than fifteen minutes at a time, twice per day. Though this is a good guideline for many, high energy and high drive puppies may not get enough mental or physical stimulation under this program. If you have concerns about how much you should be exercising your puppy, it's best to talk to your veterinarian, who may be able to recommend an exercise regimen based on your individual puppy's health and fitness. Always allow your Doberman puppy to set his own limits. If he gets tired after 30 minutes of playing with other dogs, you can let him play that long, but don't expect him to hike with you for hours at a time. Most puppies know how much they can handle and will be clear about when they're done. However, this isn't always true for high drive and high energy dogs, so again, if your puppy falls into this category, you'll need to work with your veterinarian to determine the right amount of exercise for his age.

The Importance of Mental Exercise

"Dobermans love brain games. Puppy puzzles, scent work, or games you can think up to wear out their brain a bit. Sometimes this will work to tire them out much better than a long run."

DENISE MORMAN
DeMor Dobermans

Mental stimulation is an essential aspect of Doberman Pinscher care. You need to provide your dog with daily mental exercise in order to prevent him from seeking it himself, usually through destructive behaviors. Doberman Pinschers have powerful jaws that are capable of quickly destroying furniture and personal belongings, so you must be willing to keep your Doberman busy with regular mental stimulation. Of course, mental stimulation by itself won't prevent your dog from developing bad habits, but it will reduce your Doberman's urge to entertain himself by destroying things around him.

Photo Courtesy
of Samantha Whited
Premier Dobermans

Mental stimulation is especially important for Dobermans with mobility issues or those that must have their exercise limited for health reasons, such as puppies or senior dogs. By increasing your dog's daily mental exercise, you can help make up for your dog's inability to withstand strenuous physical exercise. Mental games, puzzle toys, and training sessions are great ways to keep your dog's mind active without putting too much stress on his body. If you're interested in competition, scent work can also be a great way to compete with a dog with limited mobility.

It's important to remember that mentally stimulating activities

will wear your Doberman Pinscher out much faster than simple physical activity. A fit and healthy adult Doberman may be able to hike, walk, or play all day without ever seeming to run out of energy but may need a break after just 15 minutes of learning a new command. This is completely normal, but you need to remember to keep your training sessions short and simple to prevent mental exhaustion. If you're training new concepts, it may be best to focus on one or two new concepts per session if possible. If your dog seems to be getting confused or exhausted, it's best to go back to something that he knows well and end the session on a positive note. Pushing your Doberman beyond the limits of his mental endurance is a recipe for frustration.

Playtime

No matter how old your Doberman Pinscher is, play is a great way to keep his mind and body active. Plus, it's an excellent stress reliever to help him cope with vigorous training sessions, competition, or changes at home. All dogs have their own preferences when it comes to play. Your dog may enjoy playing alone, with their human, or with another dog. Some dogs will play at every given opportunity, and others may only enjoy play on occasion. Regardless, play is a valuable opportunity to keep your dog busy and focus his energy on an activity that he enjoys.

Photo Courtesy
of Jamie Adkins

If your Doberman Pinscher is the type to play by himself with his favorite toy, you might consider giving him a puzzle toy filled with tasty treats. Puzzle toys are great for dogs with limited mobility and often feature a variety of flaps, cups, and sliding pieces that must be navigated to find the food hidden inside. They can be made out of either wood or plastic and come in varying levels of difficulty so that you can challenge your dog more as he gains experience with puzzle toys. You can use treats or even your dog's daily portion of kibble inside the toy. Filling a Kong toy with treats is also a great way to keep your dog busy by himself. To increase the challenge, consider freezing the contents.

Many Doberman Pinschers enjoy playing with a canine companion, rather than entertaining themselves with their favorite toy. If you don't have any other pets at home, consider setting up a playdate with another dog that you know and trust. Playing with other dogs is not only great exercise, but it's also great for socialization. However, you need to be cautious about what dogs you allow your Doberman to play with. You don't want to get him into a situation where he feels bullied or anxious as this could set back his socialization, and you'll need to work harder to overcome the trauma of a play session gone wrong. Supervision is necessary any time your Doberman is playing with a dog from another household, but it's best to make sure the other dog is as calm and friendly as yours to prevent any problems.

If your Doberman Pinscher prefers the company of his favorite humans over other styles of play, don't be afraid to get creative with how you play with him. Whether you play tug, fetch, or a game of chase around the yard, it's a great opportunity to keep you both fit and strengthen your bond. You can also play a scavenger hunt type game with him by hiding treats around your indoor or outdoor space. You can keep your dog in a different area while you hide the treats and then allow him to search the space using his sense of smell and some direction from you if necessary. Searching for treats is a great way to keep all dogs entertained, but it's especially fun for dogs with limited mobility as they can go at their own pace.

Remember, every Doberman Pinscher is different, so you need to experiment to find what type of play works for your individual dog. It might be best to avoid spending tons of money on new toys and play equipment until you know your dog better and understand how he likes to play. That new squeaky toy might end up collecting dust while your Doberman wrestles with the dog next door. No matter what type of play your Doberman enjoys, you should encourage him to enjoy himself while he exercises his mind and body.

CHAPTER 16
Grooming

"A huge benefit to owning a Doberman is there is a minimal amount of grooming in comparison to other working breeds like the Bernese Mountain Dog or other heavily coated breeds. They are essentially a wash and go breed! Your dog will need to be bathed when dirty, but frequent bathing will strip the essential oils from the coat and can cause dry skin and itching. Typically, a wipe down with a damp cloth is sufficient. When a bath is required it is important to use a dog safe shampoo that is non-irritating to the eyes. You should pay special attention to not get water in his ears, but should give his ears a good wipe out once the bath is done."

TRACY DOTY
Halo Dobermans

Coat Basics

In terms of grooming, the Doberman Pinscher is a relatively low-maintenance breed. Their short, sleek coat can be maintained with occasional brushing and bathing only when needed. Though the coat may not seem like much, it serves as a thin layer of insulation and is designed to protect the dog from both the heat and the cold. A Doberman's coat should never be shaved. Not only is it unnecessary, but it can be harmful as you are removing the dog's only layer of protection from the elements.

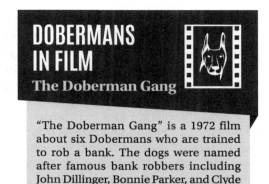

DOBERMANS IN FILM
The Doberman Gang

"The Doberman Gang" is a 1972 film about six Dobermans who are trained to rob a bank. The dogs were named after famous bank robbers including John Dillinger, Bonnie Parker, and Clyde Barrow. Three sequels followed this film in 1973, 1976, and 1980.

Doberman Pinschers are average shedders, and most will shed consistently throughout the year with little seasonal change. To minimize the amount of hair found around your home and keep your Doberman's coat in top condition, brushing is recommended two or three times per week. This is not a time-consuming activity and can typically be completed in just a few minutes. Baths are recommended every 8 to 12 weeks, but this schedule may vary according to your dog's individual needs.

Essential Grooming Tools

"Dobermans should have short nails to keep their feet the 'cat foot' as described in the standard of the breed. A toenail grinder (Dremel) is the best tool for the purpose."

PAMELA DEHETRE
Pamelot, Reg.

Regardless of whether you plan on grooming your new Doberman Pinscher yourself or sending him to a professional groomer, it's helpful to have a few grooming tools on hand to maintain his coat. The most important item you'll need is a quality brush to help remove dead hair and stimulate blood flow in the skin. For smooth-coated breeds, there are many types of brush that will work well, but many owners find a rubber curry brush to be the most effective. They can be used during the dog's bath to help distribute shampoo and remove dirt and oil from the coat, or they can be used on a dry coat between baths.

Deshedding brushes may also work, but it's important to use them with caution as it can be easy to scratch the dog's skin or damage the sleek coat. If you're unsure of what brush is best for your dog, you may need to try out a few options to determine which one you like best. You can also ask your local groomer for advice on how to keep your Doberman looking and feeling his best between professional grooms.

If you are willing and able to bathe your Doberman at home, you'll want to invest in a high-quality dog shampoo. The exact type of shampoo you should buy will depend on your new dog's skin condition as well as your own likes and dislikes. Oatmeal or medicated shampoos are ideal for dogs suffering from seasonal allergies or other skin problems. For dogs with healthy coats and no skin issues, you might choose your dog's shampoo based on the scent. When shopping for shampoos, it's best to avoid products with an excessive number of chemical ingredients. Shampoos with more natural ingredients are less likely to irritate your dog's skin, but many are considered to be low-sudsing shampoos. This just means that you'll see fewer bubbles while bathing your dog, but don't worry, he's still getting cleaned.

Conditioners are optional and whether you use one will again depend on your dog's coat condition. Dogs with dry or brittle coats may benefit from a moisturizing conditioner, while those with skin problems may be soothed with oatmeal or medicated conditioners. However, conditioner does frequently cause the coat to take longer to dry, so many owners choose to forgo this step on dogs with healthy coats. If you like the idea of conditioner but don't like waiting around while it sits on your dog's coat in the bath, you might also consider buying a leave-in conditioner that can be sprayed on after your dog's bath.

Finally, if you decide to tackle the challenge of trimming your Doberman's nails yourself, you'll need to invest in a high-quality nail trimmer or grinder. Most groomers recommend scissor style trimmers over guillotine style trimmers. Scissor-type nail clippers make cleaner cuts and do not carry the same risk of crushing the nail as guillotine type trimmers. However, more groomers are choosing to use nail grinders over trimmers when possible. Grinders are ideal for maintaining short nails but can be time-consuming if a significant portion of the nail must be ground down each time. This also puts excess wear and tear on the device, so if you opt for a grinder, it's best to use it frequently. Many dogs also prefer this method, though it may take some getting used to in the beginning. Nail grinders can be either corded or cordless, whichever appeals to you. Whether you choose a trimmer or grinder is completely up to you, but if you're unsure of the correct usage of either tool, consult your vet or groomer for advice on how to safely maintain your dog's nails.

Bathing

"I actually encourage my puppy people not to bathe their Doberman but more than once every six months. When you bathe your Doberman you actually strip the natural oils from the coat which will make the skin dry and smelly. I actually tell people to use a 50/50 mixture of blue Listerine and water in a spray bottle misted onto the coat and wiped with a dry cloth to keep them clean and nice smelling."

SHARON DUVAL
Kettle Cove Dobermans

While most groomers will recommend bathing your Doberman Pinscher every 8 to 12 weeks, that frequency will vary according to the health of his coat as well as his lifestyle. Some dogs may need weekly medicated baths to treat their skin conditions, while others may need more frequent baths simply because they get dirtier than the average dog. If your Doberman prefers to stay clean, he may be able to go longer than 12 weeks between baths. It's not recommended to bathe your dog any more often than necessary as it can dry out the skin and coat, resulting in irritation and dandruff. If bathing is not done frequently enough, dirt, oil, and dead hair can build up and cause irritation and skin problems as well.

The most important aspect of bathing your Doberman Pinscher is ensuring that the shampoo reaches the skin and doesn't just clean the top of the coat. Many groomers and owners choose to use a rubber curry brush to accomplish this. The rubber brush will help distribute shampoo evenly while also aiding in the removal of dead hair and skin cells. Most dogs also find the massaging action of the brush to be relaxing.

While shampooing your Doberman, you need to be cautious around your dog's delicate areas. Avoid getting the shampoo in his eyes and ears. If you're using a rubber curry brush, you may also want to avoid bony areas such as the legs and face. Some groomers recommend placing cotton balls in dogs' ears prior to bathing to help prevent excess water from running into the ear canals, but if you choose to use this method, you'll need to remember to remove them after the bath is done. If you're worried about getting shampoo in your dog's eyes, you might also consider having eye rinse available. If you are careful, you should be able to avoid getting shampoo and water in your Doberman's eyes and ears without much effort.

After you've thoroughly shampooed your Doberman Pinscher's coat, you need to rinse out the shampoo. If left in the coat, shampoo residue can cause hot spots and irritation, so it's crucial that you completely rinse all shampoo from the coat. Most professional groomers live by the rule that once you think the coat has been rinsed, it's best to rinse once more just to be sure. If you're using a rinse-out conditioner, you'll need to repeat these steps to ensure that all conditioner is rinsed from the coat.

When drying dogs after a bath, professional groomers typically use a high-velocity dryer to help separate the coat and dry everything down to the skin. Since Doberman Pinschers do not have a thick coat, a high-velocity dryer can dry a dog quickly, while also helping to remove the dead skin and hair that may still be intact after the bath. This method of drying isn't necessary,

Photo Courtesy
of Núria Gort Luna

however, as most Dobermans will dry quickly using either a handheld dryer or just a towel. If you do choose to use a handheld dryer, make sure you always keep one hand on your dog to make sure the dryer isn't too hot on his skin. Many dogs complete their bath with a celebratory, high-speed lap around the house, so if you don't want hair and water shaken all over your home, be sure to get your Doberman as dry as possible before releasing him.

Brushing

Despite the low maintenance of the Doberman Pinscher's coat, it's still recommended to brush your new dog one to three times per week. Most Dobermans shed consistently throughout the year, so you won't need to worry too much about seasonal coat changes. However, regular brushing will help to keep your Doberman's coat looking sleek and shiny while also keeping your home as hair-free as possible. You should begin brushing your dog as soon as possible after you bring him home for the first time to get him used to brushing. After the initial unease of something new wears off, most dogs come to enjoy this time with their owner.

For sleek coated dogs like the Doberman Pinscher, a rubber curry comb is one of the best tools to remove dead hair and skin cells while also stimulating blood flow to the skin. With this type of brush, you should be careful with how much pressure you use while brushing. You need to use enough pressure to remove hair, dirt, and dander, but not so much that you risk scratching the skin or causing discomfort or pain. If you've never used this type of tool before, consider asking your local groomer for advice. Most groomers are happy to help their clients keep their dogs looking and feeling their best.

Cleaning Eyes and Ears

When basic ear hygiene is neglected, it puts your Doberman Pinscher at risk of developing painful ear infections. Ear infections typically occur when moisture enters the ear canal. This happens frequently during bathing and swimming. Combined with your dog's natural body heat, the moisture in the ear creates the ideal environment for yeast and bacteria to grow and thrive. Dobermans with cropped ears may be less at risk than those with uncropped ears due to increased airflow in the ears. However, regardless of whether your dog's ears have been cropped, ear care remains an essential part of the grooming process and should be done on a regular basis.

Your Doberman Pinscher may have an ear infection if you notice him scratching one or both ears or frequently rubbing his ears on the floor or furniture. You may also notice redness, swelling, or even an unpleasant odor inside his ears. If you suspect that your dog may have an ear infection, it's important to take him to the vet as soon as possible for a proper diagnosis. There is no effective at-home treatment for ear infections, so the vet will need to determine whether the infection has been caused by yeast or bacteria. Treatment will vary according to the type of infection present, but ear infections are typically treated with either topical ointments or oral medications.

To clean your Doberman Pinscher's ears at home, you really only need two items: ear cleaner and cotton balls. There are two types of ear cleaners available, so you'll need to decide which is best for your dog. Some ear cleaners contain alcohol, which is great for post-swim or -bath ear cleaning as it helps to dry the ear canal. Ear cleaners with alcohol can cause a burning sensation on already infected or sensitive ears. If your dog has infected or sensitive ears, you may want to consider an alcohol-free ear cleaner instead.

Cotton balls are best for ear cleaning as they clean effectively without harming the structure of your dog's ears. Cotton swabs are not recommended as they can reach deep into the ear canal, potentially causing injury and permanent damage. Using only your fingers and cotton balls, it's nearly impossible to damage your dog's ears, so that's why they're the cleaning tool of choice.

When you're ready to clean your Doberman Pinscher's ears, wet a cotton ball with ear cleaner and squeeze out the excess liquid. Then, insert the cotton ball into the ear and gently wipe around. You can wipe around the inner surface of the ear leather as well as the ear canal itself. Don't be afraid to clean as deep as your finger can reach but use caution so that you don't cause discomfort. If your dog is currently dealing with an ear infection, his ears may be particularly sensitive, and he may react badly to rough handling. Once you've cleaned away all visible grime and ear wax, it's helpful to go over the ear again with a dry cotton ball to help dry the ear and absorb excess cleaner. This will help prevent your dog from wiping ear cleaner all over your furniture or flooring.

Tear stains are not a common issue for Doberman Pinschers, so it's unlikely that you'll need to clean your dog's eyes frequently. If you do notice a sudden increase in tearing, it's best to take your dog to the vet rather than trying to treat the issue at home as it may be a sign of a more serious eye problem. It's completely normal for dogs of any age to develop small amounts of crust or discharge near the corners of their eyes, so you may need to wipe this away on occasion. Most of the time, this discharge can be cleaned with a soft cloth, but you may also consider using an eye cleaner. Eye cleaners come in either a liquid or pre-soaked pad form and are safe for use around the eyes. However, use caution as you wipe around your Doberman's eyes so that you don't accidentally poke or scrape his eye with either the cloth or your fingers.

Trimming Nails

"The most important part of grooming a Doberman is keeping his nails trimmed adequately. This should be started when the puppy is young so that he becomes acclimated to you handling his feet."

TRACY DOTY
Halo Dobermans

Regularly trimming your Doberman Pinscher's nails is a crucial part of the grooming process. Nails that are left untrimmed can grow long enough that they can affect your dog's gait and damage his musculoskeletal structure, especially if he's still young and growing. There is no single best nail trimming schedule, so you'll need to regularly evaluate your dog's nails to determine if they need trimmed. Some dogs' nails simply grow faster than others. Dogs that are walked on pavement rather than dirt trails or grass may wear their nails down naturally and need less frequent trims. For some owners, weekly nail trims will keep their dog's nails short and comfortable, while others may only need to be done once a month.

The first step in trimming your Doberman's nails is to locate the quick, which is the nail's blood supply. You need to locate the quick so that you don't trim the nails too short, which can cause pain and bleeding. If your Doberman Pinscher has light-colored nails, the quick will be easy to see, but most Dobermans have dark nails, so it may not be as simple. To find the quick on dark-colored nails, you'll need to trim the nail in thin layers and keep an eye out for a dark-colored circle in the center of the nail. This circle is the end of the quick, and if you continue to cut or grind, you're going to go too far. As you repeat this process on each nail, it's important not to forget your dog's dewclaws if he has any.

Nail trims are relatively easy with a well-trained dog, but they can be a hassle for some owners, so if you'd rather have a professional do it, your local groomer or vet would be happy to help. Nail trims are typically inexpensive and cost less than $20 in many places. Some vets and groomers will do walk-in nail trims, but some may require an appointment, so it's best to call ahead and ask. Most professionals also offer the option of either clipping or grinding the nails, so if you prefer one method over the other, be sure to ask. If your dog is nervous or inexperienced with nail trims, professionals are often better at handling difficult dogs and calming them down, so the nail trim will be over more quickly and easily than it would with the average dog owner. After a few visits to the vet or groomer, your dog may begin to understand that nail trims aren't a big deal, and you may be able to take over if you choose to do so. If you have any questions about trimming or handling techniques, your vet or groomer may be able to show you the best way to trim your Doberman's nails.

Brushing Your Dog's Teeth

While regular professional dental cleanings are a must, so is maintaining your Doberman Pinscher's dental health at home. It's important to understand that if you are interested in brushing your dog's teeth, you must be prepared to do so every day. Consider your own teeth and how they might look if you only brushed your teeth once a week or month rather than on a daily basis. Depending on your dog's diet, tartar can build up quickly and cause dental health issues in a short period of time, so even if you aren't interested in brushing your dog's teeth, you need to check them often. Periodontal disease is painful and can affect your Doberman's ability to eat. Bacteria present in plaque and tartar can enter the bloodstream and infect vital organs. Tooth loss is also a common result of neglected dental health. Thankfully, canine dental disease is preventable with frequent at-home care and regularly scheduled veterinary checkups.

If you don't already have a toothbrush and toothpaste for your Doberman, you'll need to take a look at the selection available at your local pet store or favorite online retailer. Some dog toothbrushes will look similar to the one you use each day, but there are also other styles available, including ones that slide over your finger. There is no single best style, so you'll need to decide which type is best for you and your dog. If you aren't convinced that your Doberman won't bite down on the toothbrush once it's in his mouth, it may be best to avoid the type that fit over your finger. You might also consider buying a children's toothbrush as they are often an appropriate size and softness for use on dogs. However, you must never use toothpaste formulated for human use as it may contain ingredients that are toxic to dogs. You should be able to find different flavors of doggy toothpaste, including beef, chicken, and even vanilla. If you're the DIY type, you can also make toothpaste out of baking soda and water.

The first time you approach your Doberman Pinscher with the toothbrush and toothpaste, you may not be able to brush all of his teeth, but you shouldn't rush the process to avoid frightening him or stressing him out. To start, you'll want to put a bit of toothpaste on the toothbrush and just allow him to lick it off before trying to touch his teeth with it. Once he seems comfortable with the toothbrush and interested in the flavor of the toothpaste, you can gently lift his lips up and softly scrub each tooth in about the same way you would brush your own teeth. Do not brush too vigorously, as you may make your dog uncomfortable. Be sure to encourage patience with lots of verbal praise.

No matter how frequently you brush your Doberman Pinscher's teeth at home, you'll still need to take him to the vet for regular dental check-ups. Depending on your dog's age and health, most vets recommend dental cleanings every six to twelve months. Healthy adult dogs typically need less frequent dental care, while seniors and dogs with health problems may need to be seen more often. Your veterinarian will be able to give you a more accurate recommendation after evaluating your Doberman. Professional dental cleanings are a safe and simple procedure that require your dog to briefly undergo anesthesia. If you have any concerns about anesthesia or the procedure itself, be sure to mention it to your veterinarian.

When Professional Help Is Necessary

You don't need to struggle with grooming your Doberman Pinscher before you seek professional help. Some owners simply prefer not to groom their dogs at home, and that is perfectly reasonable. Whether your dog is well-behaved or inexperienced with the grooming process, groomers are experts in handling and gaining a dog's trust. They regularly take the most wild and unruly dogs and teach them to stand patiently for the grooming. Once your Doberman Pinscher

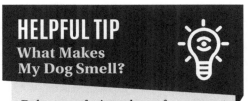

HELPFUL TIP
What Makes My Dog Smell?

Dobermans fur is made up of an overcoat and an undercoat. The soft undercoat is where the "dog" smell comes from, so you'll want to make sure to comb this coat regularly to remove excess buildup of fur and dander. Dobermans don't usually have a strong odor, but an occasional bath with mild soap will help to keep both the over and undercoats clean and odorless.

gets to know his regular groomer, he may eventually see his spa day as something to look forward to. If you are unable or unwilling to groom your Doberman yourself, paying a groomer to help maintain your dog's coat and nails may be the best choice. Just be sure to include grooming costs in your budget and don't forget to generously tip your groomer for his or her hard work, even if you're just taking your Doberman in for nail trims.

CHAPTER 17
Basic Health Care

Visiting the Vet

Depending on your Doberman Pinscher's age and overall health, it's important to visit the vet at least every six to twelve months. Though it seems silly to take your healthy dog to the vet so often, it's crucial for him to have regular checkups with a veterinarian. These checkups will allow veterinary staff to catch any problems before they can harm your Doberman's health. Many health conditions progress quickly, so it's important to identify them as soon as possible. Additionally, your dog will need regular vaccinations, dental exams, and deworming. Regular vet visits will also give you the opportunity to keep track of your dog's weight and ask any questions you may have about your dog's health or body condition. If you're unsure of how frequently you should schedule these visits, your vet will be able to provide an accurate timeline for checkups based on your Doberman's age and health.

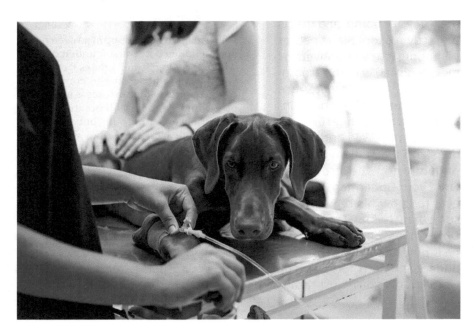

Holistic Alternatives

Many dog owners are seeking more natural lifestyles and holistic health alternatives, both for themselves and their beloved pets. If you are interested in holistic veterinary care for your Doberman Pinscher, you may want to find a holistic veterinarian in your area. Holistic vets attend the same universities as traditional vets and will treat pets with the same therapies you would find at clinics across the county. However, holistic vets are also willing to use alternative treatments such as acupuncture, nutritional therapy, and massage. With dogs who are dealing with chronic conditions, holistic veterinary care can be particularly beneficial. Whether the condition has been difficult to treat with traditional treatments or the results of those treatments aren't as significant as they should be, holistic care may be able to help.

DOBERMANS IN FICTION
Checked

Checked, a 2018 novel written by Cynthia Kadohata and illustrated by Maurizio Zorat, follows 12-year-old Conor, a hockey player who values hockey above almost everything else. When Conor's Doberman, Sinbad, is diagnosed with cancer, Conor decides to forego his hockey lessons so that his family can afford Sinbad's chemotherapy treatment. Without hockey in his life, Conor's perception of the world, and himself, begins to change. This emotional tale about a boy sorting out his priorities in life is geared towards young readers.

The main difference between holistic and conventional veterinary medicine is that holistic veterinary medicine treats the body as a whole rather than focusing on the specific part of the body that requires treatment. A common example is the dog that suffers from seasonal allergies. A traditional veterinarian may treat the problem with injectable or oral medications and possibly a medicated shampoo to help with itching. A holistic veterinarian may also use these treatments, but they may also prescribe dietary changes or herbal supplements to improve the dog's overall health. Rather than focusing only on the dog's reactions to seasonal allergens, a holistic treatment plan seeks to improve the dog's health and wellbeing in order to address the specific issue at hand.

If you are interested in taking your Doberman Pinscher to a holistic veterinarian, browse the list of vets on the American Holistic Veterinary Medical Association website. The website lists all holistic vets in the United States and Canada and can be searched by species as well as specific treatments. This will help you to narrow down your options in order to find the right veterinarian for your Doberman's specific needs.

Photo Courtesy of Collin and Kayla Williams

Allergies

Allergies are one of the most common health issues faced by dogs of all breeds and sizes. In most cases, allergy symptoms do not appear in dogs under six months of age. Most dogs are not diagnosed until after at least one or two years of age. Though experts believe that some allergies have a genetic component, most allergies are simply the result of a hypersensitivity of the immune system. Dogs can be allergic to any allergen in their environment, but the most common are food, plants, insects, and other pets or animals.

The exact symptoms of allergies will depend on the type of allergen, but the most common symptoms are localized or generalized itching, coughing, sneezing, and watery eyes. Vomiting and diarrhea are also common symptoms of food allergies. Since food allergens enter the body through the digestive system, that is typically where the reactions can be seen, though generalized itching is also common. Allergies to insects or plants are often more localized, and symptoms can be seen in the areas of the body that were exposed to the allergen. Allergens that are inhaled, such as pollen, may also cause respiratory symptoms.

Canine allergies, known as atopy, can be difficult to treat unless the allergen is known, and diagnosis can be difficult, so it's crucial that you practice patience while working with your veterinarian to determine the cause of your Doberman's symptoms. Most dogs are exposed to so many potential allergens in their environment and food that it can take time to narrow it down. If your dog is allergic to a single protein in his food, for example, you may need to feed him an elimination diet for several weeks or even months to determine which protein is causing the problem. Environmental allergies may be treated with injectable or oral anti-inflammatory or anti-histamine medications. Medicated shampoos and ointments may also help soothe itchy skin.

Without treatment, your Doberman's allergies may cause serious skin irritation and inflammation, hot spots, and hair loss. If your dog ever appears to be having trouble breathing, it's important to seek veterinary treatment as soon as possible.

Fleas and Ticks

Though fleas and ticks are common occurrences, it's crucial to seek treatment as soon as possible because external parasites can carry an array of dangerous diseases that could potentially be transmitted to your human family members. Fleas are carriers of tapeworms and bartonellosis and can cause severe anemia. Flea allergy dermatitis is also possible and can cause severe itching, skin irritation, and hair loss. Depending on where you live, your local ticks may be carrying Lyme disease, ehrlichiosis, babesiosis, or Rocky Mountain spotted fever. To keep your canine and human family healthy and disease free, regular flea and tick prevention is essential.

The exact frequency of your flea and tick prevention will depend on the climate you live in. Some climates may deal with fleas and ticks year-round, while others may only require prevention in the warmer months. Talk to your veterinarian about the best product and schedule based on your climate and the parasites present in your area. If you plan on boarding your Doberman Pinscher or taking him to doggy daycare, you may require proof of prevention prior to dropping your dog off, so be sure to ask about this when scheduling your dog's stay.

Most flea and tick prevention products come in disposable plastic vials that can be broken open. The liquid contained in the vials is typically applied to the back of the neck where the dog cannot scratch or lick it off. Although Doberman Pinschers do not have thick coats, it may be helpful to part the hair a bit to ensure the product reaches the skin. Generally, flea and tick prevention should be administered every four to six weeks.

Flea and tick collars are also an option, but most experts recommend against them. Many contain tetrachlorvinphos, which is considered to be a carcinogen by the Environmental Protection Agency. It can cause serious reactions, especially in cats. Hair loss, skin irritation, vomiting, and diarrhea are common reactions. Seizures and death are also possible.

Internal Parasites

Unfortunately, external parasites like fleas and ticks are not the only parasites that you need to protect your Doberman Pinscher from. Internal parasites, mainly worms and protozoa, are a common occurrence, so regular deworming will be required to prevent them from affecting your dog's health. As with external parasites, the specific parasites and diseases that your dog may potentially be exposed to will vary according to the area in which you live. Some internal parasites are also zoonotic, which means may also be transferred from animals to humans.

The most common internal parasites found in dogs are intestinal worms. Puppies, in particular, are prone to intestinal parasites, which they usually acquire from other dogs in the home. Worms are ingested by the puppy when it consumes water, food, soil, or feces that are contaminated with eggs or larvae. The most common intestinal worms found in dogs of all ages are roundworms, hookworms, tapeworms, and whipworms. Depending on where you live, your Doberman may also be at risk of ingesting protozoa such as giardia or coccidia.

Your Doberman Pinscher's digestive tract isn't the only system in danger of parasitic infection. Heartworms are a type of internal parasite found in the bloodstream and heart that are transmitted by mosquitos, which carry them from animal to animal as they feed. Unfortunately, heartworms are not as easy to treat as intestinal worms, and treatment can often take several months. While undergoing heartworm treatment, the dog must remain on kennel rest as strenuous activity that gets the blood pumping can result in the dead and dying parasites blocking vital arteries. If left untreated, heartworm infections can be fatal. Thankfully, heartworm infections are preventable with the use of a monthly chewable tablet.

It is possible that a dog infected with parasites may not show any symptoms at all, so frequent screening and deworming are recommended. Common symptoms of parasites may include unexplained weight loss, lethargy, vomiting, diarrhea, and coughing. Adult dogs and puppies with heavy parasite loads may have a distended belly with an otherwise malnourished appearance. Anemia is also common with severe parasitic infections.

If you suspect your Doberman Pinscher may have internal parasites, your vet will be able to detect them with a simple test. For intestinal parasites, your vet will collect a small fecal sample, which will then be examined under a microscope. The vet will be able to see the eggs, larvae, and adult parasites and determine what type of parasites are present. Once the parasites are identified, the correct treatment can be prescribed. For heartworm, a blood sample will need to be collected. The sample is then mixed with a chemical solution and placed into a disposable testing device. Results are typically available after ten to fifteen minutes or so. Treatment for internal parasites usually consists of either injectable or oral medication and can take from several days to several months to complete. Though you can't prevent your Doberman from ingesting parasite eggs and larvae, you can prevent a serious infection by scheduling regular parasite screenings and administering dewormer at your vet's recommended intervals.

Vaccinations

No matter how old your Doberman Pinscher is, he will need to be vaccinated at some point in his life. Vaccines are typically divided into two categories: core and non-core. Core vaccines, like rabies, distemper, and parvovirus, are given to adult dogs every one to three years. Non-core vaccines such as leptospirosis and Bordetella are optional but often have a shorter period of efficacy than core vaccines.

Core vaccines protect against the most common diseases encountered by dogs and are usually combined into a single syringe. The most common core vaccine is called DHPP, or five-way, and protects against distemper, parvovirus, parainfluenza, hepatitis, and adenovirus cough. Puppies are given the DHPP vaccine at six, twelve, and sixteen weeks of age. As previously mentioned, adult dogs are given this vaccine every one to three years. The frequency of administration will depend on both local laws and your veterinarian's recommendation.

The rabies vaccine is the only vaccine required by law in the United States. It cannot be given prior to 16 weeks of age and must be administered by a veterinarian. Regardless of a dog's age when it first receives the vaccine, it's generally only good for one year but may be given up to every three years after that.

Non-core vaccines are those that protect against less commonly encountered diseases. They may also include vaccines that are only effective for short periods of time, such as six months or less. Examples of non-core vaccines include leptospirosis, rattlesnake venom, Lyme disease, and kennel cough. If you board your Doberman Pinscher often, or take him to the groomer, you may be required to give him a Bordetella vaccine before you will be allowed to drop him off. The Bordetella vaccine protects against kennel cough and generally needs to be readministered every six months.

Allergic reactions to vaccines are rare but not unheard of. Symptoms of an allergic reaction include hives, lethargy, swelling of the face or paws, and vomiting. Swelling or pain near the injection site may also be possible. Severe reactions can also include difficulty breathing and seizures, and immediate treatment will be necessary. For dogs that are sensitive to vaccines, it's recommended to give only one vaccine at a time to hopefully reduce the severity of the reaction.

If you're not yet familiar with how your Doberman Pinscher will react to vaccines, you might consider staying in or near the vet clinic for around twenty minutes so that you're close enough to seek help if needed. Should your Doberman have a severe reaction to his vaccines, immediate treatment could save his life.

If you don't want to vaccinate your Doberman Pinscher as frequently as your local laws require, you may consider looking into titer testing. In some areas, titer testing may be a legal alternative to yearly vaccinations. Titer tests are performed by testing a blood sample for antibodies for the diseases in core vaccines. If your Doberman's antibody levels are adequate,

Photo Courtesy
of Barbara Higginbotham

you can skip the vaccine until a later date. If his antibody levels are too low, he will need to be vaccinated to ensure that he is protected against disease. Titer tests aren't usually available for non-core vaccines as they aren't effective for a long enough period of time to justify titer testing. Titer tests may also be more expensive than vaccines, but they are a safer alternative for dogs that experience severe reactions.

Pet Insurance

As pet owners seek ways to mitigate the costs of their beloved pets' healthcare, pet insurance is rising in popularity. There are many companies that offer a variety of policies suitable for dogs of all ages and breeds. Each

Photo Courtesy of Jessica Pilgrim

company and plan will feature different levels of coverage and cost, so it's crucial to research each plan thoroughly to make sure it's suitable for you and your Doberman Pinscher. As with human health coverage, it's possible that some dogs will cost more to cover, or they may be denied coverage entirely due to their age or preexisting conditions.

Unlike human health insurance, pet insurance typically only covers emergency veterinary care rather than preventative care. Your Doberman's annual exams, vaccinations, and deworming will have to be paid for out of your own pocket, so even if you have pet insurance, you'll still need to budget accordingly. There are some companies that offer coverage for preventative care, but it's often quite expensive. If your Doberman is injured in an accident or suddenly becomes ill, pet insurance can be helpful in covering the costs of emergency veterinary care.

Pet insurance isn't right for everyone, and many pet owners are divided on whether or not the costs of the monthly premiums are worth it. Those that have benefited from their coverage swear by it and would never go without it. Owners of relatively healthy and injury-free dogs may choose to save their money each month instead. If you aren't interested in buying pet insurance and are on a tight budget, you may want to consider saving a small amount each month so that you have it if an emergency trip to the vet should occur. If you would like to purchase pet insurance, do your research on the company that offers the plan as well their different types of coverage to make sure that you're buying the right insurance policy for your Doberman Pinscher.

CHAPTER 18

Health Concerns in Doberman Pinschers

Genetic Testing

Doberman Pinschers are a healthy breed, but there are a few health concerns that can be found in the breed. Although not all health problems can be predicted, genetic testing is an excellent way of ensuring that a breed remains as healthy as possible. Reputable breeders want to make sure that they are breeding to improve the Doberman Pinscher breed as a whole, so they're willing to spend up to several thousand dollars on genetic testing to ensure that they aren't passing any diseases on to the next generation. Less reputable breeders, however, will often overlook genetic

Photo Courtesy
of Sofia Edholm

testing and instead focus on dogs with certain coat colors or physical traits to maximize their profit.

Genetic testing is often performed by collecting a sample of your dog's blood or saliva and submitting it to an appropriate laboratory for analysis. After the sample has been analyzed, the results are evaluated by the breeder, who will then determine whether the dog is suitable for their breeding program. Reputable breeders will also submit the results of their testing to the Canine Health Information Center to be made

FUN FACT
Doberman Pinscher Health Foundation (DPHF)

The Doberman Pinscher Health Foundation (DPHF) is a 501(C)3 non-profit organization and is dedicated to raising funds for Doberman health research. The Officers and Directors of DPHF work voluntarily and aim to promote the longevity and health of the breed. In 2017, DPHF awarded its first research grant to the Michigan State University College of Veterinary Medicine for $7,500.

available to the public. Once the information is publicly available, the breeder can make it clear to everyone that their dogs are as healthy as possible, and they have nothing to hide. If you are interested in breeding your Doberman Pinscher in the future, it's crucial to have genetic testing performed to make sure you are contributing quality genetic material into the breed's gene pool. If you don't test your dog for genetic disorders, you aren't actively working to better the breed as a whole and will not be considered a reputable breeder.

Hip Dysplasia

Hip dysplasia is a common and painful condition in large and medium-size breeds. This disease can be either inherited or caused by environmental factors like injury or poor nutrition. Hip dysplasia occurs when the ball and socket of the hip joint do not fit together correctly. Instead of sliding smoothly, the joint may rub or grind, further wearing down connective tissue and eventually leading to a full loss of function of the joint.

Symptoms of hip dysplasia include lameness, stiffness, a reluctance to jump or run, and decreased range of motion of the hip joint. Affected dogs may also have atrophied thigh muscles or a unique hopping gait. Though these symptoms may strongly suggest a diagnosis of hip dysplasia, X-rays must be performed to confirm. Treatment for affected dogs will vary according to the severity of the condition, but some combination of dietary changes, physical therapy, medication, or surgery is typically prescribed.

Dilated Cardiomyopathy

"It is important to have a good relationship with your veterinarian and have routine cardiac workups done on your Doberman. Early discovery of cardiac disease and proper medications can help extend the quality of life of your companion. You should check for new bumps or lumps and have your veterinarian assess those."

TRACY DOTY
Halo Dobermans

Dilated cardiomyopathy (DCM) is a disease of the heart in which the walls of the heart become thin. As the walls stretch, the heart enlarges, and the ability to generate pressure to pump blood throughout the body is diminished. Though there are many possible causes for DCM, it is suspected to have a genetic component as some breeds are more prone to developing this condition than others. Doberman Pinschers are among the breeds with the highest rates of DCM.

Symptoms of dilated cardiomyopathy may be either progressive or sudden in onset and can include rapid breathing when resting, restless

Photo Courtesy of Tayla Jade

sleeping, weakness, fatigue, coughing, and depression. Affected dogs may have a reduced tolerance for physical activity and may suddenly collapse or faint. Sudden death is also possible as the thinning walls of the heart can lead to cardiac arrhythmias. DCM is diagnosed with the use of X-rays and echocardiograms. A combination of tests is usually required to determine the severity of the heart's condition.

Treatment for dilated cardiomyopathy will vary depending on the severity of the condition and may include oral medications such as diuretics, cardiac glycosides, and vasodilators. Treatment must typically be quite aggressive as the disease progresses quickly. Unfortunately, there is no guarantee that treatment will improve the condition of the heart or lengthen the dog's life expectancy. With treatment, some Dobermans may live as few as three months after diagnosis, while others may go on to live for as long as 24 months or more. Affected dogs that display clinical signs of heart failure are less likely to survive for long periods of time than those that are prescribed medication during the early stages of the disease.

Von Willebrand's Disease

Von Willebrand's disease (vWD) is a bleeding disorder caused by a deficiency in a certain protein that helps platelets in the blood to form clots. Approximately 30 breeds of dog are known to carry von Willebrand's, but the Doberman Pinscher has the highest incidence. In a research study, about 15,000 Dobermans were tested for the gene responsible for this disorder, and approximately 70% were found to be carriers. Most of the dogs tested did not show signs of the disease, but the gene for vWD was detected. Dobermans are by far the most commonly affected breed, but fortunately, they frequently have the mildest form of the disorder.

Von Willebrand's disease is not usually detected until about four years of age. Some dogs may be diagnosed without ever showing any symptoms. For others, symptoms include hemorrhaging from the nose, bladder, oral mucous membranes, or vagina. Affected dogs may also bleed excessively after injury, giving birth, or surgery. Death is a possibility for dogs with von Willebrand's disease if bleeding is not controlled.

Your veterinarian can test for von Willebrand's disease using a test called the buccal mucosal screening time. The buccal mucosa is the lining of your dog's cheeks inside his mouth. A small incision is made in the buccal mucosa, and the time until clotting is recorded. A normal range for the test is between two and four minutes, but dogs with vWD will have a longer bleeding time. Genetic testing will also show if an individual dog is either a carrier or affected by the disease.

Dobermans affected with vWD should not be given drugs that may interfere with normal blood clotting, such as aspirin and heparin. In an emergency, dogs with von Willebrand's disease may require blood transfusions. However, in most cases, affected dogs will not require any treatment unless they require surgery or are injured.

Autoimmune Thyroiditis

Hypothyroidism is a disorder of the thyroid gland in which the thyroid does not make enough of the hormone thyroxine. Thyroxine is the hormone responsible for controlling the metabolism. The most common cause of hypothyroidism in dogs is called autoimmune thyroiditis. Autoimmune thyroiditis is not a life-threatening disorder, but it can cause symptoms such as obesity, hair loss, and skin disorders.

Autoimmune thyroiditis varies in onset, but most dogs are diagnosed between two and five years of age. Diagnosis can be performed with a simple blood test. Treatment for the disease is usually quite easy and inexpensive and typically includes a daily oral medication.

Progressive Retinal Atrophy (PRA)

Progressive Retinal Atrophy (PRA) is a genetic disorder of the eye that is found in a variety of dog breeds, including the Doberman Pinscher. The condition affects the photoreceptors of the eye, but it is not a painful condition. There are two types of PRA: retinal dysplasia and late onset. Retinal dysplasia is usually diagnosed in puppies at around two or three months of age. Late onset is not diagnosed until adulthood, usually between three and nine years of age. With the early onset form of PRA, the photoreceptor cells are usually malformed at birth and will lead to blindness at a young age. Late onset PRA is when the photoreceptor cells develop normally but degenerate as the dog ages. Though PRA is not painful, it is a progressive disease and will get worse over time. Eventually, affected dogs will lose their eyesight entirely. For most dogs, it takes about one to two years after onset for the dog to completely lose their vision.

One of the most noticeable early symptoms of PRA is night blindness, so if you notice your Doberman Pinscher struggling to navigate in the dark or bumping into things at night, you may want to make an appointment with a veterinary ophthalmologist. Unfortunately, there is no treatment for PRA. Some research suggests that antioxidant supplements may help to slow the deterioration of the photoreceptor cells; however, there is not yet any solid proof that they work. Affected dogs typically live happy and otherwise healthy lives as they quickly learn to function without eyesight. Dogs rely heavily on other senses anyway and will be able to navigate familiar territory without any trouble.

Since PRA is a genetic disorder, it is detectable through genetic testing. Dogs affected by PRA should not be bred as they can and will pass the condition on to their offspring. Responsible breeders regularly test their breeding stock for PRA prior to being bred to ensure that they are doing their part to reduce the frequency of this disease in the Doberman Pinscher breed.

Preventing Illnesses

Although not every disease that may affect your Doberman Pinscher is preventable, proper management of your dog's lifestyle, nutrition, and healthcare will help ensure that he lives a long and happy life. As your Doberman's caretaker, it is your responsibility to provide him with a quality, balanced diet, regular physical and mental exercise, medical care, and grooming.

One of the most crucial aspects in preventing illnesses is scheduling regular veterinary appointments for your Doberman Pinscher. Though it may seem unnecessary to take a perfectly healthy dog to the vet every six to twelve months, it's essential in catching certain conditions early and providing treatment as soon as possible. There are many serious health conditions that can progress rapidly, so it's important to catch them in their early stages. Frequent checkups also give you the opportunity to ask your vet simple questions that would not otherwise warrant a vet visit. You might consider asking questions about his weight, diet, fitness, or even behavior. During these checkups, you will also be able to keep your Doberman current on all of his vaccinations and parasite prevention treatments.

Photo Courtesy of Melissa Copling

CHAPTER 19
The Aging Doberman Pinscher

Basics of Senior Dog Care

As a medium to large breed of dog, Doberman Pinschers are generally considered to be 'seniors' at around seven years of age. Of course, this doesn't mean your Doberman will wake up with gray hairs on his muzzle on the morning of his seventh birthday. It just means that this is the average age at which you may begin to notice obvious signs of aging. Some dogs may slow down before their seventh birthday, while others may act like puppies for many years to come. According to the American Kennel Club,

Photo Courtesy of Trish Norton

Doberman Pinschers have an average lifespan of 10 to 12 years, so you can generally expect to see signs of aging somewhere around the age of seven.

The changes associated with age may appear so slowly that you don't immediately recognize them at first. Your aging Doberman may begin to take longer naps or get tired more quickly during physical activity. He may also have difficulty getting out of bed in the morning, or he may struggle with stairs. Some dogs may also experience a deterioration in their hearing or vision, so you may need to be more careful around him to avoid startling him. Many older dogs also have changes in weight as their metabolism and appetite changes. Some may gain weight, while others become quite thin. It's also common for senior dogs to require more frequent trips outdoors as their bladders may not be as strong as they once were. Another common symptom of aging is cognitive dysfunction, or dementia, which typically arises in the form of behavioral changes or temporary confusion. As the signs of aging become more obvious to you, you'll need to adapt your Doberman's care and environment to accommodate his changing needs.

Regular Vet Visits

"I believe preventing injury while they are younger is important to keeping a healthy senior. Always monitor your dog for limps, aches, and pains. They will generally be very subtle. Dobes are very stoic. Often by the time you know something is wrong they are very injured or ill."

DENISE MORMAN
DeMor Dobermans

You may need to take your senior Doberman Pinscher to the vet more frequently for checkups than you did when he was in his youth. Though many adult dogs are fine with a once-yearly checkup, many vets recommend checkups for seniors at least every six months. Changes can happen quickly during the senior years, so it's important to catch any problems as soon as possible. Many older dogs also experience a decline in dental health, so they may require more frequent dental cleanings as they age.

At these checkups, you may want to talk to your veterinarian about any recommendations he or she may have for your dog as he ages. Your Doberman may benefit from changes in diet or exercise, or he may need certain medications to help him cope with the common conditions of old age, such as arthritis. Any sudden change in weight or behavior may also require attention, so don't be afraid to mention them to your vet at your dog's next visit.

Nutritional Changes

"You may want to begin moistening his kibble with warm water to make it a bit softer and easier to chew. Keeping your Doberman in good weight is imperative in his senior years as aging joints cannot easily support an overweight dog. Switching him to a senior food may assist in his caloric intake while still keeping him full."

TRACY DOTY
Halo Dobermans

For many senior dogs, the metabolism changes related to aging will require changes in their daily diet. An active adult Doberman Pinscher may be able to consume a relatively high number of calories without gaining weight, but many senior Dobermans may need to have their calories reduced to maintain a healthy weight. Though there are many health risks associated with obesity, excess weight can be particularly painful for senior dogs dealing with arthritis. That pain can lead to reduced mobility and even more weight gain if left unaddressed. Portion sizes must be adjusted to accommodate your aging dog's nutritional needs. You should also consider switching your Doberman Pinscher to a senior dog food, as senior food often contains fewer calories per cup with the addition of helpful ingredients such as glucosamine, chondroitin, and MSM.

If you notice that your aging Doberman Pinscher seems to be losing weight rather than gaining it, you're not alone. Weight loss is common with older dogs as they develop health problems or changes in their appetite. Finding a food that appeals to these picky eaters is crucial in maintaining their weight. Whether that means changing their diet entirely or just adding tasty toppers will depend on your dog's preferences. If your Doberman Pinscher has been eating the same kibble for his entire adulthood, you may want to consider switching brands or adding in canned food. You can also try changing to or supplementing with raw or cooked food.

Some senior dogs will also develop health problems that require a change of diet. Dobermans that have developed kidney or heart problems will require a prescription diet rather than a normal food from the pet store. You may also want to give your dog nutritional supplements for his joints like glucosamine, chondroitin, MSM, or green lipped mussel. Senior dogs dealing with digestive problems may also benefit from the addition of probiotics, fiber, or digestive enzymes. During your Doberman's senior years, any sudden changes in your dog's weight, appetite, or stools should be addressed as soon as possible. It's important to talk to your vet to rule out any health problems before making major changes to your Doberman's diet.

Photo Courtesy of Rebecca Menapace and Joe Gross

Photo Courtesy of Nataliya Volkova & Justin Bowley

Exercising Your Senior Dog

"With age your Doberman will begin to slow down. You will want to continue your exercise routines and walks, but making them shorter and let him determine how long he wants to fetch as he will tire more easily now."

TRACY DOTY
Halo Dobermans

As dogs age, their metabolism begins to slow, and some may develop arthritis. This means you may notice your Doberman Pinscher becoming less enthusiastic about strenuous physical activities. He may opt for an afternoon snooze on the sofa rather than his usual afternoon hike through the woods. While you shouldn't eliminate all physical activity from your Doberman's daily schedule, you do need to adjust it to accommodate his changing body. Exercise is essential to good health, but you may need to make do with shorter walks or low-impact activities like swimming.

As strenuous physical activity begins to be more challenging for your Doberman, you might consider substituting more mental exercise in its place. Mentally stimulating activities are ideal for senior dogs to keep them busy and engaged without overstressing their bodies. For many seniors, their body slows down long before their mind, so mental challenges like scent work or puzzle toys may be right up their alley.

To keep your aging Doberman Pinscher safe during exercise, you may also want to find new places to exercise. Hard surfaces such as pavement, slick floors, and long flights of stairs pose a risk to older dogs who are more likely to become injured. If your home or neighborhood allows, try exercising your Doberman on soft grass or carpeted flooring instead of concrete or hardwood floors. The softer surfaces will help keep your dog comfortable, and the change of scenery will be a welcome adventure for him.

HELPFUL TIP
Longevity Program

The Doberman Pinscher Club of America (DPCA) will award the Longevity Certification (LC) to Dobermans who have lived to age 10 or older, or who have parents who have lived to age 10 or greater. This award may be bestowed posthumously. Records of Dobermans who have been awarded the LC are kept in a database maintained by the DPCA. For more information about the requirements for this award, visit the DPCA website.

Environmental Changes

"The primary concern for an aging dog is what accommodations you can make to help make his senior years comfortable. Consider adding non-slip rugs on hardwood floors and creating him an area where he doesn't have to go up and down stairs or provide an outdoor ramp. He's given you his best years of love and devotion and there is an obligation to provide him comfort during his golden years."

TRACY DOTY
Halo Dobermans

In addition to exercising your Doberman in new locations, you may also need to adjust your home environment to adapt to your dog's changing needs. Many dogs lose their strength as they age, and they may begin to find stairs and slick flooring to be physically challenging. Keeping their balance may be more difficult than it once was, and they may be at risk of falling. Consider changing your décor a bit to suit your dog by adding baby gates at stairs and non-slip rugs on slick floors. You might also consider having your dog wear non-slip socks or booties to help him get a grip. There are also harnesses available to enable you to assist your dog up long flights of stairs if needed.

Some senior dogs will also experience cognitive changes, and they may appear confused or lost at times, so you need to ensure your aging Doberman won't be able to get himself into trouble. Stairs, pools, and outdoor spaces can all pose a risk to a confused senior dog, so you may need to limit his access to such areas. If your Doberman Pinscher is used to sleeping on the furniture, you may need to provide him with pet stairs or a comfortable lower alternative. Some of the changes suggested in this section may not complement your existing décor, but it's important to prioritize the comfort and wellbeing of your aging Doberman.

Preparing to Say Goodbye

Though it may be a difficult time to think about, there will come a time when you will need to begin planning for the end of your Doberman Pinscher's life. In some cases, the end may come sooner than expected, so it's important to be prepared. Remember, when planning to say goodbye, you need to keep your Doberman's quality of life in mind. If your beloved dog no longer enjoys his favorite activities or his suffering outweighs his happiness, it may be time to say goodbye. As you prepare, it's essential that you reflect on your favorite memories that you shared together. These memories can help you navigate your grief during this difficult time.

For many people, it can be difficult to determine whether or not your Doberman Pinscher is ready to say goodbye. Your dog's quality of life should always be prioritized, but there are a few key things to consider. Here are some questions to ask yourself about your dog when making decisions about his quality of life:

- How often does your dog require assistance with mobility? Some of the time or every time?
- Is the dog taking pain medication, and does it make a difference in his pain levels?
- Does your dog still have a healthy appetite?
- Does your dog ever have episodes where he struggles to breathe?
- Is your dog able to control his bowels and bladder, or does he frequently have accidents?
- Does your dog still enjoy spending time with his favorite people or pets?

If your dog no longer seems to care whether he's being petted, is in pain most of the time, is unable to stand by himself or control his bowels or bladder, struggles to breathe, or has lost his appetite, it may be time to talk to your vet about humane euthanasia. Each pet is different, so it's important to consider your Doberman's overall quality of life when making these decisions. If you're unsure, your veterinarian may be able to help you make the right choice.

When the time comes to say goodbye to your Doberman Pinscher, it may be too stressful to really make many decisions, so it's helpful to make plans in advance, so you know what needs to be done and can focus on your final moments together. Many veterinarians offer in-home and in-office euthanasia services, so you have a choice of where you'd like to say goodbye. Some owners may find it difficult to say goodbye in an unfamiliar exam room, while others may prefer not to have the memory of saying goodbye in their own home. Whichever you prefer, you might consider discussing your options with your vet as the time nears. No matter what, the most important aspect of your goodbye is that you are with your Doberman as he passes over the rainbow bridge. He will be comforted knowing that his final moments in this world are spent with his favorite person or people.

Euthanasia is a painless procedure administered by a licensed veterinarian that ensures that your beloved companion does not suffer. The vet intravenously administers an overdose of an anesthetic called sodium pentobarbital. The drug is typically administered while the dog is lying down so that it can be safely injected into a vein, usually in one of the front legs. If the dog is frightened, confused, or in pain, a sedative may be given first to relax the dog. After the sodium pentobarbital enters the bloodstream, the dog is unconscious within seconds, and the heart is stopped in less than a minute. The veterinarian will confirm that the dog has passed by listening for a heartbeat with a stethoscope.

After you've said goodbye to your Doberman, your veterinarian may offer you different options for your dog's remains. If you would like to take your Doberman's remains home for burial, you will be able to do so. If you can't bear the thought of dealing with the remains yourself, your veterinarian will be able to make the necessary arrangements for disposal for an additional fee. Most clinics also offer cremation, and you should be able to decide whether you'd like the ashes returned to you. Cremation is usually done at a separate facility, so be aware that it may be several weeks before your dog's ashes are returned to you. It can be helpful to explore your options in advance so that you're prepared when it's time to make the decision. Different clinics offer different options, so you'll need to discuss the matter with your vet if you don't already know what you'd like to do.

Photo Courtesy of Megan Revels

Grief and Healing

The first few days and weeks after losing your Doberman Pinscher are the hardest, but it will get easier with time. You are not alone in your feelings. Everyone who has had the blessing of sharing their life with a beloved dog knows what you're going through. It can be helpful to reach out to friends and family during this stressful and emotional time. Some owners also choose to create a memorial for their pets. Many artists and companies offer personalized jewelry, garden décor, and tiles to memorialize your Doberman. You should consider volunteering in your community as a way to distract you from your grief and help other people or animals. Consider planting trees or gardens in your dog's memory or make a donation to a breed rescue or other organization. Helping others can help some owners navigate their grief.

Everyone handles grief differently, and some people may struggle more than others. If you find that you are struggling with your grief or can't seem to move on, you should consider contacting a grief counselor or mental health professional. Many people lack the necessary coping methods to get through this difficult time, and professional advice can help you process your feelings. No matter how you deal with the feeling of loss, it's important that you cherish the memories you shared with your Doberman Pinscher and the feeling of unconditional love that you received.

Made in United States
Troutdale, OR
09/10/2023

12807321R10110